$Sacramental$
REFLECTIONS

Sacramental REFLECTIONS

Feasting at the Lord's Table

TRUMAN G. MADSEN

DESERET
BOOK

Salt Lake City, Utah

Visit us at DeseretBook.com

Library of Congress Cataloging-in-Publication Data

(CIP data on file)

ISBN 978-1-62972-022-7

Printed in the United States of America

Edwards Brothers Malloy, Ann Arbor, MI

10 9 8 7 6 5 4 3 2 1

To the many deacons
who thought I was asleep

And to the few who knew
I was never more awake

CONTENTS

FOREWORD

When we had been married about three weeks, I remember bewailing the fact to my wise husband, Truman, that I took the same small sins to the sacrament week after week. I was trying hard, then harder, to improve but made no progress. It changed my life forever when he said, "Honey, it's not just about gritting your teeth and trying harder. You can never do it alone. You come to the sacrament to ask the Lord to help you, to lend you his strength, to add it to your own. He can make weak things strong! You're not supposed to do it alone."

Some years later, I wrote the following poem while sitting in a sacrament meeting:

The Sacrament Prayers

The words are repeated
once again
this sacred, Sabbath time.
Words I can trace
through the week
but this time
unique,
spoken quietly
in youthful
intonation,
and the nourishment
is proffered
to me

by a boy's hand
in exchange
for
my changing.

When I shared the poem with my twelve-year-old grandson, Max, who was about to be ordained a deacon, I asked him if he understood it. He said he did and then explained, "I have the privilege of taking fruit from the tree of life and giving it to the members of my ward—and I get to eat it too." He understood in much the same way his grandfather always had, and he taught me in that moment.

Truman's legacy has enriched our family and come full circle in our posterity. For sixty years he tutored me in his tender way, always bringing me a step closer to the Savior. He taught me to remember more.

Many of Truman's inspiring insights about the sacrament have been gathered in this book. It was one of his last projects before he passed away in 2009. I'm thankful for the opportunity it gives me—and you—to reflect on what he gathered in a lifetime of learning how better to feast at the Lord's table.

ANN MADSEN

PREFACE

While the Jerusalem Center was still under construction, an admiring architect said, "Whoever speaks in this room must be either very profound—or silent."

He was standing with me in the "upper room" of the Jerusalem Center, built to frame and focus a panoramic view of the golden city. In that very room in a sacrament meeting—I remember the chair he was sitting in—was a reluctant visitor.

He was by his own description "a former member." After years of participating in the Master's cause, he now found himself out of the Church. For an equal number of years he had been flintlike in his resistance to all efforts to bring him back.

He was here under protest. With his partners he had traveled on business to a nearby country. Then they had quietly booked a flight to the Holy Land. He almost felt like he had been kidnapped to attend this meeting.

He sat looking over to the golden city, dimly aware, as he later told me, that out there within that vista Jesus had lived the last week of his life. Soon it was hard not to think of the last hours.

Whatever the hymns, the prayers, and the emblems meant to him, something grasped him and shook him. Within that profound and silent hour his defiance melted away. He was malleable and repentant. He became absolutely resolute to return. "I must go home and, whatever it takes, start over with Christ."

And so he did.

This is one of many "moments of truth" I witnessed during five years in the Holy Land. Just such moments have led to this little volume.

After glimpse upon glimpse of the sites and sights of Jesus's life, and after line upon line of probing sacred texts, I have written these impressions. They are here combined with snippets of real-life records, ancient and modern, to show how some of the most trustworthy disciples have woven the sacrament into the very fabric of everyday life.

The idea was to produce a handy and carry-able booklet. It has now expanded. As it turns out, each page completes one main idea and can stand on its own. There is no fixed beginning or end. It need not be read in sequence, but can be "dipped into" at random. All italics in quoted materials have been added unless indicated otherwise.

In the old world, in the new, and in the living present, Jesus has given his sanction, his authority, and his power as he has introduced the sacrament.

Sooner or later we will learn the shining truth. He himself has said it applies to all of us, "in all cases under the whole heavens" (D&C 52:19).

It is this: he can fully reach us, and we him, only if we obey his ordinances (see D&C 52:16).

His sacrament ties together in us all other ordinances.

"This shall ye always observe to do, even as I have done. . . . And it shall be a testimony unto the Father that ye do always remember me. And if ye do always remember me ye shall have my Spirit to be with you" (3 Nephi 18:6–7).

TGM
Brighton, Utah
Summer 2007

Atonement

AT THE UPPER ROOM

Standing here amidst the hollow echoes of ancient limestone walls are Elder David B. Haight and his wife, Ruby. We are in the vicinity, if not the exact room, of the Last Supper on Mount Zion.

He speaks softly to us. Hospitalized after a rupture in his aorta, he was clinging to life and unconscious. During this crisis he was given a vivid dream-vision of Jesus's last week on earth. Now, gratefully recovered, he is anxious to see this site. We listen almost breathlessly:

> I heard no voices but was conscious of being in a holy presence and atmosphere. . . . The first scene was of the Savior and his apostles in the upper chamber on the eve of his betrayal. Following the Passover supper, he instructed and prepared the sacrament of the Lord's Supper for his dearest friends as a remembrance of his coming sacrifice. It was so impressively portrayed to me—the overwhelming love of the Savior for each. I witnessed his thoughtful concern for significant details—the washing of the dusty feet of each apostle, his breaking and blessing of the loaf of dark bread and blessing of the wine, then his dreadful disclosure that one would betray him.[1]

Then followed the Savior's solemn discourse when he said to the eleven: "These things I have spoken unto you, that in me ye might have peace. In the world ye shall have tribulation: but be of good cheer; I have overcome the world" (John 16:33).

Elder Haight presses his finger to my chest and his eyes are alight: "We do not appreciate the sacrament enough. It happened. It is real. It is our access to the Savior." The same affirmation is in Ruby's eyes.

---

1. Haight, "The Sacrament—and the Sacrifice," 59–61.

THE SPEAR AND THE VOICE

The aged Simeon somehow knew by the Spirit that before his own death he would be privileged to see the Messiah.

It happened in the temple. He held the infant Jesus and said to mother Mary, "This child is set for the fall and rising again of many in Israel, and for a sign which shall be spoken against" (Luke 2:34).

Then came apprehensive words:

"Yea, a spear [the King James says a 'sword'] shall pierce through thy own soul also, that the thoughts of many hearts may be revealed" (JST, Luke 2:35).

This was the mother who later "stood by the cross" (John 19:25). The mother who witnessed the piercing of hands and feet and then of the spear to the wounding of her "own soul also," who heard his cries to the Father—and heard him say, "Woman, behold thy son" (John 19:26).

If the human heart can think as well as feel, then in this recital crucial thoughts are born in us also. Our most revelatory moments occur when we are pierced to our core.

The Spirit is razor-sharp and cuts to the quick.

We are taught: "My word . . . is quick and powerful, sharper than a two-edged sword, to the dividing asunder of both joints and marrow" (D&C 6:2; 11:2; 12:2; 14:2).

Elsewhere, the voice is not a loud voice, it is "a pleasant voice, as if it were a whisper" (Helaman 5:46). Yet it goes to our very center and causes our hearts to burn (see 3 Nephi 11:3).

Elsewhere: "[The] word . . . of Jehovah has such an influence over the human mind [the logical mind] that it is convincing without other testimony. Faith comes by hearing."[1]

We can learn to listen at all times and places and vibrate like a tuning fork. But we may hearken best when we are in holy places performing holy ordinances.

---

1. *Words of Joseph Smith*, 237.

HOW LONG IS AN HOUR?

In the time of Jesus, there was a small but cultured town known as Sepphoris—"jewel" or "ornament." It became a Roman capital of Galilee. Jesus's home at Nazareth was only a few miles from Sepphoris.

In Sepphoris eighty years before Jesus's birth, a Hasmonean army took terrible revenge on a rebel uprising by a "massive live crucifixion."[1] When Jesus was in his teens, one account says, hundreds of rebels were crucified, with their wives and children slaughtered before their eyes.

Reports of these crucifixions surely would have reached Jesus. He may even have conversed with witnesses. The Romans possibly required their subjects, including Jesus's father, Joseph, and his apprentice son, to provide some of the crossbars or stakes.

In any case, the shadow of crucifixion reached Jesus early. Did it bring apprehensions to his heart? How early did he realize he was to be "the Lamb slain" in this way? In maturity, at a wedding celebration in Cana, near Nazareth, Jesus said to his mother (the first time he used the phrase), "Mine hour is not yet come" (John 2:4). "Hour" in Greek can mean a segment of a day, but it may also mean a definite period of time, often tied to the seasons—"the hour" of fall, for example, or of winter.

Three years later, as the hour approached, he cried out in recoil, "Now is my soul troubled; and what shall I say? Father, save me from this hour." Shortly—how long later?—he cried out, "But for this cause came I unto this hour" (John 12:27). His incredible prayer of submission followed: "Father, glorify thy name.

"Then came there a voice from heaven, saying, I have both glorified it, and will glorify it again. The people therefore, that stood by, and heard it, said that it thundered: others said, An angel spake to him. Jesus answered and said, This voice came not because of me, but for your sakes" (John 12:28–30).

Yes, "his hour," long anticipated, finally came for our sakes.

---

1. Josephus wrote in *Antiquities* 13:14:2 that in 88 BCE, the Hasmonean king, Alexander Jannaeus (in office 103–76 BCE), ordered the crucifixion of 800 Pharisees.

WHY IS THIS NIGHT DIFFERENT?

If the Passover order that has endured through millennia was followed that night, the youngest son or daughter was to stand and say so all could hear, "Why is this night different from all other nights?"

For the rest of the evening, and often past midnight, the songs, the narratives, the repetitions, the symbolic gestures and partakings are the answer. This is the night we (never "they") were delivered from slavery, from Egypt, from Pharaoh, when God passed over the children of Israel.

Part of the seder is to rehearse the series of miracles. Having been part of a spectacular deliverance from the sea, the people are shortly murmuring about the hardness of the desert and the plainness of the fare. So God performs a daily small miracle. He feeds them—from heaven. He delivers to them just enough, sufficient (*dayenu*). And two portions over the Sabbath.

On this night in the upper room, the youngest person present, if tradition prevailed, was John: John who in the reclining posture put his head without protest on the bosom of the Master. The lovable disciple of love.

The climactic answer that night was again deliverance—this time from the mouth of the Deliverer. He now fed them in anticipation of giving himself.

Did they comprehend that he was about to be betrayed into a judicial travesty? That he would not resist arrest, nor plead in his own defense, nor answer baiting questions, nor scheme to escape by simply walking into the desert from Mount Olivet?

Such a night—the darkest and yet most illuminating night in history. Such a moon—the brightest moon in the year. Such a sun—a searing sun, a merciless sun, soon to beat upon the Son of Righteousness.

COMFORT AMIDST DOOM

Jesus introduced the sacrament in the midst of disciples who could have been beyond consoling. All prospects were grim:

- I am about to go away.
- You are soon to be hounded and hated as I have been.
- One of you is going to betray me.
- The rest of you will be scattered and driven.
- You may have to lay down your lives.
- You will be helpless without me.

Yet in the midst of this he gave spiritual reassurance:

- I will be gone, but the Spirit will come to sustain you.
- If you understood, you would rejoice at my departure.
- I will not leave you comfortless. (In Greek, "I will not have you orphans.")
- I will meet you again in Galilee.
- Someday we will be together at the wedding feast.
- You feel alone, separate, bereft. But listen to my prayer: we can be one.
- " . . . as thou, Father, art in me, and I in thee, . . . one in us" (John 17:21).
- You need teaching; you will have it by the spirit of truth.
- You need life; I have it to give.
- Let not your hearts be troubled.
- Remember, I have overcome the world.

His disciples wept in a swirl of emotion.

GETHSEMANE:
WAS HE ABSOLUTELY ALONE?

As we walk near the gnarled olive trees in the Garden of Gethsemane, we are confronted by a small sculpture etched into the wall. It depicts Jesus kneeling at what appears to be a rough-hewn altar.

We are gripped by a sense of total exhaustion. Christ's body not only kneels but stretches out under the weight upon him—drawn, spent, limp, anguished, writhing under the strain.

We have been taught that even with his inherent gifts of divine intrusion, he still could not turn this oppressive grinding millstone alone. A moment came, the record says, when "there appeared an angel unto him from heaven, strengthening him." And then "he prayed more earnestly" (Luke 22:43–44).

Out of all the panoply of heaven, who would be sent as a celestial Samaritan on this mission of mercy? Someone he knew? Someone who knew him? And how was power transmitted on that awful and tormenting night?

One truth emerges.

If he could not go it alone, neither can we—not without his strengthening us. To endure and overcome the world, our all is required. But our all is not enough. It must combine with his. Only he can lift us to the full reaches of our potential. Much in our secular society says, "Oh, yes I can. I can do it my way." But that is disabling vanity. Even the slightest needs of repentance require Christ's purifying power. And for those of us near despair who cry, "Oh no, even *with* him I cannot go through with this," he replies, "I can lift. I will heal."

That night he was stretched to reach both human extremities— to the petulant and proud and to the depressed and despairing.

A MIDRASH ON THE MESSIAH

The role and the upreaching reliance of the Messiah as suffering servant is in this Jewish midrash:

> The seven years in which the Messiah, son of David, is to come, iron beams will be brought and laid on his neck, until he is stooped and he will scream and cry, and his voice will ascend on high. He will say to him: Master of the universe, how long can my strength persist, how long my spirit, how long my soul, and how long my limbs? Am I not flesh and blood?
>
> It was for that moment to come that David wept and said: "My strength is dried up like a potsherd" (Psalms 22:16). At that moment, the Holy One, blessed be he, will say to him: Ephraim, my righteous Messiah, you have already accepted upon yourself all the suffering from the six days of Creation. Now let your sorrow be as my sorrow. For, from the day wicked Nebuchadnezzar ascended and destroyed my house, and burned my habitation, and exiled my children among the nations, by your life and the life of my head, I have not sat in my throne.
>
> At that moment the Messiah will say to him: Master of the universe, now I am content. It is enough for a servant to be like his master.[1]

Did not Jesus say to Peter at the washing of feet, "The servant is not greater than his Lord" (John 13:16)?

Did not "the Son of Man" say to Joseph in the dungeon, "Art thou greater than he?" (D&C 122:8).

---

1. Glatzer and Sloan, *Hammer on the Rock,* 109.

AND IT WAS NIGHT

After the Last Supper, the record says, "And it was night" (John 13:30). I have witnessed the effort of pious Jews as they stand—they do not kneel—at the place that is but a remnant of the wall below the ancient walls of the temple mount. Rhythmically, they throw their whole bodies into their prayers. They are sometimes ridiculed for this. In reply they say, "We are fighting distraction. We want to concentrate. Motion helps." Some pray all night long.

For Jesus, the motions of that night, I suggest, were more internal than external, and somehow the bitterness was bitter as gall. That burden, that venom, he vicariously took within. "How?" we cry out. But a child can understand. Pain hurts. Even the presence of it hurts those of us who merely observe and stand detached. The Savior, who is supersensitive—who did not take a backward step from the will of the Father—could and did feel for and with us. The pressure worked upon him.

Luke, whom tradition says was a physician, recorded that great drops of blood came from the Savior's pores (see Luke 22:44). His very body oozed. It is not a spectacle we wish to recall, but we have been commanded, weekly, however weakly, to memorialize it in the sacrament. Even then, all his preparation and all he could summon from his own strength was not sufficient. And more earnestly, says the record, he prayed, and an angel came, strengthening him (see Luke 22:43–44). Strengthening, but not delivering.

He had the power to summon legions of angels to end the ordeal. But he did not summon them.

During the same night he was betrayed, he was taken prisoner. He was broken into, pierced by scourging. One reading of Pilate's motives suggests that he hoped this public display would suffice for those who were crying out against Jesus. It did not. The weight, I submit, had begun there on the mount, a greater weight than the weight of his body that he was then to bear on the cross.

THE ANOINTED ONE

During Passover night as he knelt in the moon-shadow of the temple, which was for centuries the altar of blood sacrifice, Jesus's heart was melted and wrenched.

We are told that here the pangs and pains of sin "according to the flesh" bore down upon him and entered him that his bowels might be filled with compassion, that he might know by experience so unfathomable that no human case could fall outside the circle of his care.

"According to the flesh" he came to comprehend how to succor his people "according to their infirmities," for he subjected himself to all our feelings—the guilt, the abandonment, the despondency and despair—that go with them (Alma 7:12–13).

When he emerged from Gethsemane he was in the complete sense the Messiah, the Anointed One (in Greek, *Christos)*. He had been "beaten for the light" (Leviticus 24:2, "to cause the lamps to burn continually"). The cross would be the final seal of his unspeakable suffering. But from that early-morning hour he was fully the Light of the World. As he had testified in the little town of Nazareth: "The Spirit of the Lord God is upon me; because the Lord hath anointed me" (Isaiah 61:1; cf. Luke 4:18). Though the world knew it not, he was anointed by his own blood, and as he descended below all things, he became the servant of all.

[He was a servant because he sought to exalt all humankind—any and all who would come forward to him.]

Oil press for light

10

LAW AND THE INEVITABLE

We sometimes say, "There ought to be a law." We want to stop or compel this or that behavior. But law does not tell us what we *must* do. It tells us the inevitable results of what we *do* do. In the religious life, and in all of life, this is an absolute that cannot become obsolete.

If we seek our own satisfaction, indifferent to or even hostile to the law, we will reap the consequences—100% guaranteed. And if we recognize and observe the law, we will reap the consequences. Laws penalize or reward. We decide which.

"But didn't God make the laws? Can't he fix it so they no longer apply, at least to me?" From the voice of Christ himself the answer has come anew in our time: some laws are eternal and therefore irrevocable. Even by God (see D&C 130:20).

"But aren't we to receive mercy rather than justice for our maladies and malefactions? Isn't that what his amazing grace is all about?" Yes, on certain conditions. But the <u>conditions are lawful</u>.

Christ fulfilled the law. But he did not replace it. He fulfilled his part so we could fulfill our part. Here is his word: "That which breaketh a law, and abideth not by law, but seeketh to become a law unto itself, and willeth to abide in sin, and altogether abideth in sin, *cannot be sanctified* by law, neither by mercy, justice, nor judgment" (D&C 88:35).

He does not say he *will not* sanctify us. He says he *cannot.* This is not an arbitrary decree.

His grace is enabling and supportive. But it does not and cannot replace our power to act for ourselves. We must reach in the way ordained for its increase. If and only if we come to the Lord genuinely penitent, then and only then will it be just, fair, right, and good to grant us mercy, forgiveness, and healing.

"Unto none else"—except the truly penitent—"can the ends of the law be answered" (2 Nephi 2:7; also see Alma 27:18; 42:23–24).

⚹ This is the way to become entitled to the glorious dispensation of mercy: by inner change that has outer effects—forever.

ATONEMENT AS COVERING

In the Old Testament the word *kippur* or *kuppuru* is translated as "atonement." The word has three main strands of meaning:

- to cleanse or purify
- to cover—in order to hide or veil
- to smear or wipe [away] (with allusions to the temple altar)

The Prophet Joseph speaks of Christ's love—charity—as "covering" or making amends for a multitude of sins. In another translation he adds that it *prevents* a multitude of sins (see James 5:20; JST, Peter 4:8).

So three acts of love are demonstrated in Christ's Atonement:

When it means to cleanse, it fits with his command to "cleanse your hands and your feet" and "purify your hearts" in preparation (D&C 88:74; 112:28). It fits with the Lord's definition of "sanctify," and with all the "schoolmaster" requirements of diet and ritual in ancient Israel (see D&C 43:11). "Ye shall be holy: for I the Lord your God am holy" (Leviticus 19:2).

When it means to hide or veil or hinder the knowledge of, it fits with his promise that "I, the Lord, remember them [sins repented of] no more" (D&C 58:42). They will not count against us nor will they be "spoken upon the housetops" (D&C 1:3). Nor will we be asking for the mountains to cover us up from the all-searching eye of God (see Luke 23:30).

When it means to smear and wipe, it fits with the revelation that as Jesus endured purging of blood, he can enable us to emerge through cleansing treatments, until we are "clean every whit"—not only on the surface, but through and throughout our whole person, mind, spirit, body—"sanctified by the spirit unto the renewing of [our] bodies" (D&C 84:33).

Can Christ do all that for us? He can. And he will, if we will submit to treatment. One day it may be said of us as of Absalom: "But in all Israel there was none to be so much praised as Absalom for his beauty: from the sole of his foot even to the crown of his head there was no blemish in him" (2 Samuel 14:25).

CRUCIFIXION AND SECURITY

In a cave in east Jerusalem a skeleton was recently discovered. It could be dated to the first century. The man had been crucified.

The spike that penetrated both feet had struck a knot in the hard wood, perhaps heavy olive wood, and resisted withdrawal. So that part of the cross was cut off and entombed with the man. It was discovered that:

- Nails or pegs were driven through the wrists.
- The body was not stretched fully on the cross. Slack was left in the legs, which were angled sideways.
- One spike was driven through both feet.

To try to diminish the inestimable pain in the feet, the victim could shift more weight to his arms and hands. But then in agony he would shift downward. Slowly the victim would writhe and twist up and down until he was totally exhausted, until he could not even hold up his head. Struggling to breathe, he might suffocate.

If this or anything like it was the mode of Jesus's crucifixion, it is incredible that he could live more than a few hours. The gospel accounts say that Jesus died—by his own volition, and only when "it was finished"—the same day he was nailed to the cross.

Greek words for "sure" and "surety" are associated with the cross. And in and between all scriptural narratives, Jesus pleads, "Become as securely bound to me as I was secured to the cross. And you shall be lifted up at the last day."

CROSS

In the first century of the Jewish-Christian church, the signs and symbols of worship revolved around the Resurrection and the empty tomb. The iconic use of the cross came later, much later. The cross symbol with its variations has found its way into the architecture, onto the pinnacle of spires, into the amulets and paintings of Christendom.

But clearly the divine intent is to take its significance beyond our eyes into our frail flesh—whatever the outward signs. Every ordinance of the gospel presupposes and is suffused with the consciousness and centrality of both the Atonement and Crucifixion of Christ. But at the same time they signal his transcendent release from the cross and his ascent over "the last enemy," which is death (1 Corinthians 15:26; Revelation 20:12).

"And my Father sent me that I might be lifted up upon the cross; and after that I had been lifted up upon the cross, that I might draw all men unto me, that as I have been lifted up by men even so should men be lifted up by the Father, to stand before me, to be judged of their works, whether they be good or whether they be evil" (3 Nephi 27:14). The way we honor his act is in our nerves and muscles, in mind and heart, and in taking up our own cross.

The calling to "take up your cross" came from his resurrected lips, as he stood, his wounds apparent, amidst the Nephites (3 Nephi 12:30). "And now for a man to take up *his* cross, is to deny himself all ungodliness, and every worldly lust" (JST, Matthew 16:26). Nephi praises the saints who have endured the crosses of the world and says they shall inherit the kingdom of God (see 2 Nephi 9:18). D&C 23:6 admonishes us to "take up [our] cross." D&C 56:2 says that "he that will not take up his cross . . . shall not be saved."

The remembrance and intimacy of the Crucifixion is the beginning and end of dedicated temples, the center and the climax. In a sense we are to bear *his* cross—to "believe in Christ, and view his death, and suffer *his* cross and bear the shame of the world" (Jacob 1:8).

WHY NOT "THY KINGDOM COME"?

Most of us know the Lord's Prayer word for word.

Unaccountably, however, two phrases of this prayer are omitted from the sermon in Third Nephi: "Thy kingdom come" and "Give us this day our daily bread" (see 3 Nephi 13:9–11).

One possibility: A humbled—and more receptive—remnant of the people had survived cataclysmic earthquakes and were near the temple. At the outset even they were unable to hear the subtle but penetrating voice from on high (see 3 Nephi 11:3). Now, though, Jesus was in their midst and ministering and inviting them, even little children, to touch him.

The King brought with him the kingdom. He poured out authority and counsel. And, afterwards, baptisms of water and of fire.

He, the liveliest living oracle, was with them and they fully received him, hanging on every word. His teaching was not just the word of others, but the word of him who inspires the word.

Thus this Nephite multitude *became* the kingdom of God. No need to pray, "Thy kingdom come." It had come.

As for the bread, "Give us this day our daily bread" may have meant, "Give us today a foretaste of the bread we will partake of in your presence." Now he was in their presence. Tenderly he provided, miraculously he presented, the sacrament to his twelve disciples and then through them to the gathering.

Soon these Nephites were no longer neophytes. They were truly a people like Enoch's. They and their children and their children's children endured faithfully for two centuries.

Just such a multitude of authentic saints is needed to prepare and be prepared for him at the next coming. With his endowment of the Spirit they will continue in peace and righteousness, not just for days or months, but for centuries. Ten centuries.

"WHO FOR THE JOY
THAT WAS SET BEFORE HIM"

Jesus was indeed, as Isaiah foresaw, "a man of sorrows, and acquainted with grief" (Isaiah 53:3). Who more than he knew the dark tones of life!

But that is not the dominant note of his life and person. Too often it is exaggerated until his religion is distorted into something morose. That is the opposite of divine intent. John reminds us that Jesus was no Pollyanna. "He knew what was in man" (John 2:25). And clearly the sorrows and griefs that concerned him most were those of others. He came to diminish and relieve them, not to compound them. He is not a man of poison darts.

The real Jesus was and is a person of resilient gladness and sunshine, acquainted with rejoicing. We can suppose that his face shows smile lines. He was a healer of many forms of illness or distress—and filled with delight and thanksgiving for the gratitude of those who leapt for joy.

Our scriptures enable us to feel two contrasting moments when he prayed: "Father, I am troubled because of the wickedness of the house of Israel" (3 Nephi 17:14). Yet almost in the next breath, amidst a circle of cherubic children, we hear him say, "And now behold, my joy is full" (v. 20). So saying and so praying, he wept. Gladsome tears (vv. 21–22).

Almost all the occurrences of the word *joy* in the Book of Mormon and the occasions leading to it are shared joy. They come in the sharing of times of blessedness and sociality and kinship and participating with others.

Melancholy is not the name of the Savior—nor of his disciples. He lives and breathes, saying, "How great is my joy." It was that anticipation that enabled him to endure Gethsemane and the cross "for the joy [in Greek, 'calm delight'] that was set before him" (Hebrews 12:2). And he inspired an ancient prophet to say, "The joy of the Lord is your strength" (Nehemiah 8:10).

THE FACE OF THINE ANOINTED

The human face is an immediate giveaway of our feelings and mode of life. Said the Prophet Joseph, "You may always discover in the first glance of a man, in the outline of his features, something of his mind."[1]

Offering the dedicatory prayer at Kirtland—and in the wake of prayer meetings where he beheld the face of the Son—Joseph prayed about the "generation of vipers" who had driven, dispossessed, and sought to exterminate the saints (see D&C 109:47–52). He prayed that they be brought to justice (compare D&C 121:5).

But, addressing the Father, he then said: "Inasmuch as they will repent, thou art gracious and merciful, and wilt turn away thy wrath when thou lookest upon the face of thine anointed" (D&C 109:53).[2]

Exquisite wording! This is not a feeble hope but an acknowledgment of the touching truth: that as the Savior compassionately views even the most unrepentant of us, the Father honors his cry to postpone judgment. Is anything more persuasive than the face of his Son? His countenance reflects, as do the prints of the nails, his rescue mission.

In this real world of retaliation, there is ample room for condemnation. Were the Father to act on the worldly scale of anger and wrath, there would have already been a vast destructive wave.

So what restrains him? It is the infinite patience and love of his Son. He can still see gold in the corrupted mines of the worst of us, even in a vineyard that has become "corrupted every whit" (D&C 33:4).

"The Lord of the vineyard said unto the servant: Let us go to and hew down the trees of the vineyard and cast them into the fire, that they shall not cumber the ground of my vineyard, for I have done all. What could I have done more for my vineyard? But, behold, the servant said unto the Lord of the vineyard: Spare it a little longer. And the Lord said: Yea, I will spare it a little longer, for it grieveth me that I should lose the trees of my vineyard" (Jacob 5:49–51).

---

1. Cited in Woodruff, *Wilford Woodruff*, 176.
2. The "a" in "anointed" is capitalized in later editions.

The Prayers

SACRAMENTAL PRAYERS

What exactly did he do at the table that night? What exactly did he say? What exactly did he intend? The biblical record is severe in its brevity.

Through the centuries elaborate efforts by linguists, ritualists, historians, and textual critics have done their heroic best. Only to conclude that we cannot know for sure the answers to these questions.

But the Restoration has brought to the fore deep and moving clarifications. We have the words spoken by Jesus in another sacramental setting. All three questions are answered.

We are taught not to vary a word from the prayers—both the letter and the spirit of Christ's gospel is therein.

✳ As B. H. Roberts has written, "This is the only church in all the world that has a god-given prayer of consecration on the emblems of Christ's body and blood. It came from Jesus Christ, the highest spiritual authority. The Lord has spoken and the matter is ended."[1]

---

1. B. H. Roberts's remarks in Ogden, November 21, scrapbook of his daughter, Georgia Mowry.

KNEEL WITH THE CHURCH

Amidst a community of disciples in America, so Moroni wrote, "Their elders and priests administering the flesh and blood of Christ unto the church." And following the example of Jesus: *"They did kneel down with the church, and pray to the Father in the name of Christ"* (Moroni 4:1, 2).

Modern revelation likewise instructs that the priest is to kneel "with the church" (D&C 20:76). This can mean in the presence of the church. It can also mean kneeling as all others kneel. Both have occurred in our history. In our meetinghouses today, the whole congregation does not typically kneel.

But while our body is sitting, or even lying down in a sickbed, our spirit can kneel: "heart up while the head is down."

In Hebrew (for example, in Isaiah 66) the word *bawrak* ("kneel") is a synonym for "bless.' By implication, when one kneels he blesses God in an act of submission. But also the reverse: one receives by kneeling. This idea is associated with salute and praise as well as with abundance.

The scriptural symbolism is rich. Camels kneel to receive or unload their ladings or burdens. In resting places they kneel by reservoirs. Lambs kneel to be fed by their mothers. For neither water nor milk nor divine blessings flow uphill. Jesus's two Marys knelt at the feet of the newly alive Son—and clasped his knees (see Luke 24:10).

All this foreshadows a day ahead, a day in his presence. Someday every knee shall bow and every tongue confess (see D&C 76:93, 110).

Nothing so strengthens feeble knees as kneeling upon them in communion with Christ.

WHAT MAKES IT SACRED?

Orson F. Whitney taught:

"When we partake of the Lord's Supper, we bless bread and water, or the priest does it for us.

"Why so? Is there any sacred efficacy in the bread or water, taken alone? No; there is not water enough in the ocean nor bread enough in all the bakeries of the world, to constitute the Lord's Supper. What, then, makes it effective as a sacrament?

"It is the <u>blessing</u> pronounced upon it by the Priesthood and the symbolism whereby those elements are made to represent something greater than themselves, namely, the body and blood of the Savior. What is done then becomes a holy ordinance, full of force and effect, a poem in action."[1]

<u>By his priesthood Jesus is represented</u>. In another way he is presented. Because as we pray together, so does he:

> Listen to him who is the advocate with the Father, who is pleading your cause before him—saying: Father, behold the sufferings and death of him who did no sin, in whom thou wast well pleased; behold the blood of thy Son which was shed, the blood of him whom thou gavest that thyself might be glorified; wherefore, Father, spare these my brethren that believe on my name, that they may come unto me and have everlasting life (D&C 45:3–5).

---

1. Whitney, *The Strength of the "Mormon" Position,* n.p.

THE BODY TO REMEMBER

We take the bread "in remembrance of the body of thy Son . . ."
What body? We have a wisp of remembrance of his spirit body, even
though the veil has been drawn, for we saw him in premortality. "We
saw the Savior chosen and appointed" there.[1] We speak and sing much
of the infant Jesus in Bethlehem and later in the temple.

We read of the mature Jesus anointed by Mary of Bethany only days
before his death and weighed down in Gethsemane and on the cross.
Through the eyes of witnesses we envision the resurrected Jesus before
whom the two Marys knelt. And we read of the awed encounter of the
eleven with him in glory.

All these are stages of Christ's embodiment.

But he teaches that the body we are most to memorialize—to recognize and honor and, should we be so *blessed,* eventually to embrace—is
his glorified body filled with light as witnessed by the Nephite multitude. This is the body men, women, and little ones saw and were invited
to touch. We say the body was perfect. So it was. But it bore the record
of what he has done for us. Imprinted are the scars in his side and hands
and feet.

He said, "And this shall ye do *in remembrance of my body, which I
have shown unto you.* And it shall be a testimony unto the Father that ye
do always remember me. And if ye do always remember me ye shall have
my Spirit to be with you" (3 Nephi 18:7).

This is the triumphal body. This is the body of hallowed and majestic destiny. This is the full measure of divine creation. This is what
the Savior's life and death were to generate. The process could be called
"Christogenesis," the upthrust from primal element, the masterpiece
and masterwork of his and our divine Father.

Most miraculous: his glorious body is the prophecy of our own future resurrected bodies, and the body we may one day touch in a royal
embrace "encircled in the arms of his love" (D&C 6:20).

---

1. *Words of Joseph Smith,* 60.

ALL THOSE WHO PARTAKE
AND DRINK OF IT

Rarely do we take the sacrament or other ordinances alone. And rarely in an ordinance setting are we the sole beneficiaries. We say "amen" to a prayer that is a prayer for all present. And even all absent—for implicit is the hope that others soon or someday will join us in the feast.

Each prayer on the sacramental emblems prays in behalf "of all those who partake of it" or "all those who drink of it" (D&C 20:77, 79).

When we drink *of* a cup there is yet something left in the cup. When we drink a cup of something it is emptied.

Jesus has proclaimed that his cup is ever-flowing as we drink of it. His living water will "spring up to everlasting life." And we shall never thirst in vain.

All of the Lord's gifts are inexhaustible.

This is a world where we calculate, measure, and compare, where there is never enough. "If I eat, you may not; if I drink, you cannot." "The bottle is empty." "You didn't get your share."

But his promises are complete: Everyone is an heir of all—and not just some.

The treasures of eternity are in the depths of Christ's personality. The more they are received the more they are, in his pattern, given. Love is not diminished but increased when bestowed, for love generates love.

Light is not a quantity that will be detached and carried away until it runs out.

Intelligence is not spent by sharing, but grows expansively.

The truth can be taught to one or a million, and in the very teaching its influence is increased. The more who come to know, the more truth is apparent, and the more extensive its dominion.

One day truth, his shining truth, will fill the earth, and the earths, "as the waters cover the sea" (Isaiah 11:9).

NAME AND ATONEMENT

When the *Kohen Gadol* (high priest) went into the temple on the Day of Atonement, he had already undergone elaborate preparations for purification. The experience was considered awesome, even perilous. The pronunciation of the name was thought to bring him into direct contact with the divine—through the power of the name, he was able to experience God as "a consuming fire." If spoken in unpreparedness or without concentration, the name could bring dire results for him and the family of Israel.

One of the oldest passages of the Mishnah says that the high priest at the appointed place and time on the Day of Atonement offered thrice a certain formula containing the name. The congregation answered after him: "Blessed be the name of the glory of his kingdom for ever and ever."

Thus the name of the King of Righteousness became, symbolically, the name of His Righteous Kingdom and of its members. After the third recitation, "the priests and the people who stood in the Court at the time when they heard the Name, coming forth from the mouth of the high priest, bent the knee, prostrated themselves and fell on their faces and said: 'Blessed be the Name of His Glorious Kingdom forever and ever.'"

Christ has become the high priest at the appointed place. And as we take upon us his name, he promises:

"Keep all the commandments and covenants by which ye are bound; and I will cause the heavens to shake for your good, and Satan shall tremble and Zion shall rejoice upon the hills and flourish" (D&C 35:24).

HOLINESS AND THE NAME

In ancient temple times, the name of God was held so sacred that it was uttered only once a year, on the Day of Atonement, and then only by the high priest in the act of "cleansing the sanctuary"—the holy of holies. There the acts of the entire house of Israel were recorded, it was believed, as if by an iron pen. By that process, conditional on their repentance, the people were purified and granted another year of life.

For observant Jews this one name is to be remembered, but never uttered and never forgotten. They even call the Lord himself *"Ha Shem,"* the name.

Caution has been given in our time: "Let all men beware how they take my name in their lips." Because "that which cometh from above is sacred, and must be spoken with care, and by constraint of the Spirit" (D&C 63:61, 64).

We covenant in a sacrament setting that we are *willing* to take upon us "the name of thy Son" (D&C 20:77). Such willingness is the preamble to the full actualization of name-taking and covenant-taking and covenant-making. And where? In the temple. Hence, the beauty of the promise from Christ himself at Kirtland: "My name shall be here; and I will manifest myself to my people in mercy in this house" (D&C 110:7).

To forget this inscribed name of God is to forget who one is. It is to forget the very essence of belonging, to blur the meaning of one's own identity. Our name is our own past, present, and future. The name of Jesus is a prophecy. He sees our becoming as we do not and, without his Spirit, cannot. We took his name-covenant before mortality. And we renewed it again by birth and rebirth in the everlasting covenant. Now each week, by confirming our remembrance, we actualize it.

The name is transmitted and placed upon us, from our prayer. Our "amen" seals it.

OF THE MANY POWERS OF NAME

Jesus—*Joshua* in Hebrew—is one sovereign name. It relates to many other names that are also titles.

In Hebrew, combinations of consonants at the beginning or end of a word bring out enlightening variations.

So in Hebrew the word for "name" is *shem*. Often "Ha [the] Shem" functions as a reverential name of God.

Shem with a capital *S* is the name of a great high priest. *Shem* combined with *-esh* means "sun" or "light" or "fire."

Shem combined with *-mayim* means "water," water from the heavens.

Shem combined with *-en* means "oil," including the oil of anointing.

Each of these meanings Jesus embraced and embodied.

He is the great high priest, who shares with us his priesthood. He is in the sun and moon and stars, the light that proceeds forth "to fill the immensity of space" and quickens our understanding (D&C 88:12).

He is the flowing water that cleanses and turns inner deserts into fruitfulness—whether we are natural branches *or* grafted.

He is the anointed one who consecrates and bears to us the oil of healing.

Thus, as the atoning Son *Yeshua ha Maschiac* (Jesus the Anointed One), he confers and ordains, radiates and endows, washes and cleanses, anoints and heals.

He has become the preeminent prophet, priest, and king. And he lives and serves to make of us prophets, priests, and kings.

NAMING AND CALLING

In a recent science fiction account, an earthling meets an interplanetary stranger for the first time and says, "What is your name?" The stranger replies, "We have no names here. We know who we are."

The KJV says Jesus returned from his temptation to Galilee and "He taught in their synagogues, being glorified of all." The JST reads, "being glorified of all who believed on his name" (JST, Luke 4:15).

In Greek, the commandment "baptizing them in the name of the Father and the Son and the Holy Ghost" means "baptized into the name" or "incorporated into the name."

A little girl asked to pray amidst guests was naming the members of the family. She wanted to include a visitor sitting at the table but could not recall his name. She paused, opened her eyes, pointed, and said, "Him." Then closed her eyes and went on. She settled for a pronoun.

In prayer, as in daily life, there is a question: "What do I call you?" But in relation to the Savior there are more crucial questions:

"How do I call *to* you?" "How do I call *on* you?" "How do I call *for* you?"

In these cases the word or name is a summons. It invokes the person, absent or nearby. In the daily world of exchange, the right word can be a password. In various ways one can have the right to use it, the right to wear it, even the right to *be* it. "I *am* my name." Though its imprint may be invisible, there are ways of making it clear before guards or protectors at entryways. Our name, then, is our credential, our status, our power of privilege.

Even if we are wearing the uniform of the enemy, if we are named correctly, we are friend, not foe. We belong. It is a word of entitlement. And when we pray to commune with the Lord, we don't have to get through a battery of secretaries or make an appointment. As we pray in his name we have immediate admittance. We belong to him.

THE EFFICACY OF BLOOD

Without the shedding of blood is no remission of sins.[1]

In a discourse on the passage "flesh and blood cannot inherit the kingdom of God," the Prophet Joseph explained that the kingdom here refers to "the kingdom that God inherits or inhabits."

In that condition, he adds, the flesh is without blood, for the Spirit of God replaces it. Blood is the part of the body that is subject to corruption. So whether one is translated or resurrected, the blood "vanishes away."

> Therefore Jesus Christ left his blood to atone for the sins of the world that he might ascend into the presence of the Father, for God dwells in flaming flames and he is a "consuming fire."
>
> He will consume all that is unclean and unholy. We could not abide his presence unless pure Spirit [is] in us. For the blood is the corruptible part of the tabernacles. For the resurrection is devised to take away corruption and make man perfect or in the glory which he was created for. The body is sown in corruption and raised in incorruption. Then we will be able to go in the presence of God.[2]

Thus the shedding of his blood validates "the covenant of the Father" and enables us to become free of the distortions and sins, the "blood of this wicked generation" (D&C 88:75).

---

1. "And almost all things are by the law purged with blood; and without shedding of blood is no remission" (Hebrews 9:22).
2. *Words of Joseph Smith*, 371.

WINE AND BLOOD

John's Gospel is sometimes called the "Book of Signs." His intent is through and through sacramental.

Jesus turns water into enough wine—and much more—for all who attend the wedding feast at Cana. The Greek language often uses "wine" as symbolic of blood. In Gethsemane, he turned his own blood into redemptive wine.

He "wrought out this perfect atonement through the shedding of his own blood" (D&C 76:69). The virtue of his blood has become an intimate perpetual prayer: "For I am Christ, and *in mine own name, by the virtue of the blood which I have spilt,* have I pleaded before the Father for them" (D&C 38:4).

His blood and the blood of the faithful ones who follow him, some to stark trials, some to ridicule and rejection, some to daily scorn, but all to newness of life, combine into a permanent upreach—a proof of his earnest descent and ascent in our behalf.

It is written that his blood "which was shed for them" (D&C 20:79) cries unto God from "under the altar that John saw" (D&C 135:7; see also Revelation 6:9).

It cries for our forgiveness, and it cries for justice. It is a token of mortality that promises immortality. To reverse corruption, his blood must purify. "By the blood ye are sanctified," Father Adam and Mother Eve were taught (Moses 6:60). And thus the paradoxical statements that "our garments are made white"—where blood usually stains—"in the blood of the Lamb" (see 1 Nephi 12:11; Alma 5:21, 27; Alma 13:11–12; Mormon 9:6; Ether 13:10).

How do we apply his atoning blood? Through faithful and prayerful trust in him and his covenants and ordinances.

The proffered outcome in all of us is a "righteous people, without spot and blameless" (D&C 38:31).

WHERE IS THE NAME WRITTEN?

The Father calls upon us to accept the inscription of his name and the name of his Son in every vital place. Examples:

In the heart: "Ye should remember to *retain the name written always in your hearts,* that ye are not found on the left hand of God, but that ye hear and know the voice by which ye shall be called, and also, the name by which he shall call you" (Mosiah 5:12).

In our thoughts: "A book of remembrance was written before him for them that feared the Lord, and that *thought upon* his name" (3 Nephi 24:16).

In the palms of our hands: "Even unto them will I give in mine house and within my walls a place . . . *an everlasting name [a "yad vashem"], that shall not be cut off* '" (Isaiah 56:5; *yad* = hand or palm, and *shem* = name).

On the forehead: "When the Lamb shall stand upon Mount Zion, and with him a hundred and forty-four thousand, having *his Father's name written on their foreheads* " (D&C 133:18).

In our daily life: "Christ, the Son of God; and that believing ye might have *life through his name* " (John 20:31).

In a white stone: "And a white stone is given to each of those who come into the celestial kingdom, *whereon is a new name written,* which no man knoweth save he that receiveth it. The new name is the key word" (D&C 130:11).

The spiritual culmination of all these is to have our name written "in the Lamb's book of life" (Revelation 21:27), or, more precisely, the Lamb's "book of the living" (Psalm 69:28; see also Isaiah 4:3), never to be blotted out (see Exodus 32:32–33).

THE WORD "ALWAYS" AND THE ROCK

After introducing the sacrament among his twelve disciples, whom he had commanded to "sit themselves down upon the earth," and "when they had eaten and were filled" (3 Nephi 18:2, 4), the twelve disciples gave to the multitude. When the multitude were filled Jesus said (and note the use of "always"):

"This shall ye *always* observe to do, even as I have done . . . in remembrance of my body, which I have shown unto you. And it shall be a testimony unto the Father that ye do *always* remember me. And if ye do *always* remember me [in this way] ye shall have my Spirit to be with you" (3 Nephi 18:6–7).

He introduced the same pattern with the wine. First, the disciples received. Then they gave to the multitude. And they—both those who ministered and those who received from them—"were filled" (3 Nephi 18:9).

Then Jesus said:

> Blessed are ye for this thing which ye have done, for this is fulfilling my commandments, and this doth witness unto the Father that ye are willing to do that which I have commanded you. And this shall ye *always* do to those who repent and are baptized in my name; and ye shall do it in remembrance of my blood, which I have shed for you, that ye may witness unto the Father that ye do *always* remember me. And if ye do *always* remember me ye shall have my Spirit to be with you. . . .
>
> And if ye shall *always* do these things blessed are ye, for *ye are built upon my rock.* But whoso among you shall do more or less than these are not built upon my rock, but are built upon a sandy foundation; and when the rain descends, and the floods come, and the winds blow, and beat upon them, they shall fall, and the gates of hell are ready open to receive them. (3 Nephi 18:10–13)

What We Bring

OUR NEEDS

In the midst of our mortal predicament we have needs, even desperate needs. One is for a mentor, an exemplar, who has been over not just a similar road but an even far worse one. A person who can show us what we have in us to do and to become—one who is able to say to us without hypocrisy, "What manner of men ought ye to be? Verily I say unto you, even as I am" (3 Nephi 27:27).

We need a person who knows (feels) the heights and depths of our frailty, our stupidities, and our failures, no matter how extreme they become. He must be no stranger to our glaring imperfections, immaturity, and rebellions. We need one who is acquainted firsthand with all these earthly weaknesses. Moreover, as a physician of mind and body, he must know the antidotes to the poisons we have inherited and imbibed.

We need a person who is willing and able to act in our behalf, not because of compulsion nor grudgingly, but because of genuine care, rooted in love—a constant and steady love. Otherwise, how can we trust him? How can we be assured that at some point he will not abandon us, go his own way, let us down? That he will help and not exploit us?

When we run afoul of the law and violate our own best intentions and sink in the aftereffects, including guilt and torment, we need, indeed we crave, an even-handed and wise judge. But we long for him to also be merciful: one who has the right, the authority, and the ability to deliver us from the threats of bondage and the compounding of our misdeeds. He must be willing, whatever the decrees of others, to use his own resources to absolve us of severe punishment, indeed, to intervene in our behalf.

But what if that means he himself has to pay the penalty?

He will. Above all he must be willing to do the same for those whom we have injured, mistreated, misled. Is there any person in the universe who qualifies for such multiple roles? Only One.

INSPIRED INTROSPECTION

In his sacrament—and in all the other ordinances—the Lord gives us glimpses of ourselves. In self-examination we are most blessed when we begin to see ourselves as we are seen by him and know ourselves as we are known by him (see D&C 76:94). Knowledge of the Savior and self-knowledge flow together. "Let a man examine himself," Paul counseled (1 Corinthians 11:28).

Said the Prophet Joseph Smith, "We are all stimulated by a certain motive. Motive precedes action, and if we want to know ourselves this is the key, to examine the motive—what it is—and the fact will be manifest."[1]

Whatever our present soul-sicknesses, the Savior sees beyond them. He knows our glorious past—who we were in the premortal spheres. And he can and does envision our destiny and what we are to become.

In contrast, we live under the blur of amnesia of our past, and we are subject to fits of blindness and disbelief about our real potential. Said George Q. Cannon:

> Now, this is the truth. We humble people, we who feel ourselves sometimes so worthless, so good-for-nothing, we are not so worthless as we think. There is not one of us but what God's love has been expended upon. There is not one of us that he has not cared for and caressed. There is not one of us that he has not desired to save and that he has not devised means to save. There is not one of us that he has not given his angels charge concerning.
>
> We may be insignificant and contemptible in our own eyes and in the eyes of others, but the truth remains that we are children of God and that he has actually given his angels . . . charge concerning us, and they watch over us and have us in their keeping.[2]

---

1. *Words of Joseph Smith*, February 23, 1841.
2. Cannon, *Gospel Truth*, 1:2.

THE HEART OF JERUSALEM

Jerusalem, city of light, has a heart. And in it is written the story of the human family.

To this hour the city is an unspeakably powerful lure to the religious impulses of the peacemaker. But few cities in history have witnessed as much of war and laying waste.

Today as we walk the streets of Jerusalem, we see the cruelty of all this in the eyes of little children: innocence gone, inner light quashed, hope and high purpose overshadowed by the stirrings of bitterness.

One morning recently, Jerusalem awoke to ten inches of snow. Nothing like this had occurred in 100 years. Suddenly adults became children and children became themselves, filled with wonder. Enmities faded, scorn was forgotten, a new set of energies emerged. People poured out of their homes, and in their meetings and partings, in work and in travel, they threw handfuls of snow as they would throw kisses. They laughed, rolled, embraced, and jumped in a swirl of goodwill. Every human contact was humane. Celebration, sharing, and a tangible peace filled the air.

Then the snow melted and ancient tensions and conflicts resumed.

The experience proved one thing: in the most closed center of the self may lurk the capacity to be open, joyful, and humane. In the stoniest of hearts there is potential for softening. In the most strained of relationships there is the possible renewal of kinship. When we choose to see ourselves and others with new eyes—the eyes of Christ—new life, and even love, may come into us.

"FIRST BE RECONCILED"

Of the temple altar Jesus said in Jerusalem, "Leave your offering there before the altar and go; first be reconciled to your brother, and then come and present your offering."[1]

In his sermon in America it is implied that another "altar" may well be the sacrament table: "Therefore, if ye shall come unto me, or shall desire to come unto me, and rememberest that thy brother hath aught against thee—go thy way unto thy brother, and first be reconciled to thy brother, and then come unto me with full purpose of heart, and I will receive you" (3 Nephi 12:23–24).

The net weight of the Lord's requirement is to reconcile with our adversaries and forgive everyone everything every time.

No exceptions.

The phrase in the Lord's prayer, put negatively, is, "Do not forgive me one iota more than I forgive others."

"If men will smite you, or your families, once, and ye bear it patiently and revile not against them, neither seek revenge, ye shall be rewarded; but if ye bear it not patiently, it shall be accounted unto you as being meted out as a just measure unto you" (D&C 98:23–24).

What? The unforgiving victim is told that *he* deserved such treatment from the victimizer? By continuing resentment, by reviling in our mutterings, by magnifying and sometimes voicing grievances, and by striving for revenge, we are making great strides backward over the bridge of forgiveness we ourselves must cross.

On the other hand, the Savior's rewards for patient forgiveness are glittering. "An hundred-fold" (D&C 98:25). Seventy times seven multiplied. And the glory overall: our full and complete forgiveness at his hands. For "should we even forgive our brother, or even our enemy before he repent or ask forgiveness, our Heavenly Father would be equally merciful unto us."[2]

---

1. Matthew 5:24 in the New American Standard Bible, 1995.
2. *Teachings of the Prophet Joseph Smith,* 155; *Words of Joseph Smith,* 7.

OF WORTHINESS

As we approach the sacrament, we may judge ourselves too harshly. Wrote Elder Melvin J. Ballard:

> I suggest that perhaps some of us are ashamed to come to the sacrament table because we feel unworthy and are afraid lest we eat and drink of these sacred emblems to our own condemnation. And so we want every Latter-day Saint to come to the sacrament table because it is the place for self-investigation, for self-inspection, where we may learn to rectify our course and to make right our own lives, bringing them in harmony with the teachings of the Church and with our brethren and sisters. It is the place where we become our own judges. There may be some instances where the elders of the Church should properly say to one who in transgression stretches forth his hand to partake of the emblems: You should not do this until you have made restitution, but ordinarily we will be our own judges. If we are properly instructed we should know that it is not our privilege to partake of the emblems of the flesh and blood of the Lord in sin, in transgression, or having injured and holding feelings against our brethren and sisters.
>
> No man goes away from this Church and becomes an apostate in a week or in a month. It is a slow process. The one thing that would make for the safety of every man and woman would be to face the sacrament table every Sabbath day. We would not get very far away in one week, so far away but what perhaps by this process of self-investigation, rectifying the wrongs we have done, they may be corrected in the beginning. If we should refrain from partaking of the sacrament, condemned by ourselves as unworthy to partake of these emblems, we couldn't stand that long and we would soon, I am sure, come to the spirit of repentance; and so it is the path of safety for Latter-day Saints.[1]

---

1. Ballard, "The M.I.A. Slogan," 468–73.

IMAGINATION

We may not be able to fully conceive or comprehend all that happened in Gethsemane and on the cross and the resurrection.

But we can imagine.

The power of such imagination has been described by one of our leaders—Joseph Fielding Smith:

"If we could picture before us—as I have tried many times to do—if we could see the Savior of men suffering in the garden and upon the cross and could fully realize all that it meant to us, we would desire to keep his commandments and we would love the Lord our God with all our heart, with all our might, mind and strength and in the name of Jesus Christ would serve him."[1]

Hard, analytic thought has its role. But conceptual thought even at its best is fragmental. Imagination is inclusive of the whole range of human awareness, including feeling-tones.

Jesus's life and likewise his teachings are a series of images—concrete, pictorial, vivid. His parables are all imagistic—narratives, stories, using familiar objects, animals, places, things, in an unfamiliar way. His images are drenched with feeling, as if he is pleading, "Can you picture that? Can you feel that? Can you respond to that?"

His appeal to our image-making capacity requires more of us than conceptions in the mind, which can be cold and passionless.

Imagination is a prime attribute of the truly repentant and religious man. If it fails us we are spiritually impoverished and can only be "cured" by actual occasions of suffering, and then by accurate memory. For "all will suffer until they obey Christ himself."[2]

In the end, weak or insipid imagination limits our access to the Atonement. There is a saying, "If you don't know what causes me pain, how can you say you love me?" We surely know what causes him pain. So?

---

1. Joseph Fielding Smith, in Conference Report, October 1929, 63.
2. *History of the Church,* 6:312–13.

THE LOWER PART OF THE INNER COURT

A little boy ran from playing into the house, sobbing as if his heart would break. His grandfather stooped down to embrace him. "What is it?"

"I was playing hide-and-seek with my friends. I went and hid and no one came for me. They all ran away."

The grandfather encircled him in his arms. "Now you know how the Lord feels. He hides, and no one comes for him."

The Savior sequesters himself in sacred places and awaits us—he asks us to come and "stand in holy places" (D&C 87:8). His instructions on the design of the Kirtland Temple include these:

"And let the lower part of the inner court be dedicated unto me for your sacrament offering, and for your preaching, and your fasting, and your praying, and the offering up of your most holy desires unto me, saith your Lord" (D&C 95:16).

If each of us is a temple, and if the architecture and inner design of the stone-on-stone temple are recapitulated in man, then the "lower part of the inner court" in the human self is the bottom of the heart.

From that heart of hearts, not just from the top of the head, are to come our authentic sacrament offerings, preachings, fastings, and prayings. It is the locus and source of our "most holy desires" offered up to the Lord.

Such seeking is matched with his countering promise: "the heavens [shall] shake for your good" (D&C 21:6; 35:24). "And ye shall find."

We cannot hide from the Lord. He may hide from us until we reach for him from the inner part of the lower court. Then he answers.

OF PRAYER AND CONFESSION

It is told of an ancient holy man that when he prayed for his people, all the people who had ever asked him to pray for them in his long life passed through his mind in supplication. How, he was asked, is that possible? Surely there was not enough time.

He replied, "The need of every single one leaves a trace in my heart. In the hour of prayer I open my heart and say, 'Oh Lord of the world, read what is written here.'"

The holiest of such holy ones is "the Holy One of Israel," Jesus the Christ.

As our sins, our unworthy desires, our negating habits, and our secret enemies reach the fiber of our hearts, they reach the fiber of his.

To break open, to confess all that is presently locked within us, is sometimes a dreadful exposure. But this very exposure is the beginning and the continuation of His curative power in us. Diagnosis must precede therapy.

Hence as he says in modern revelation: "For I, the Lord, require the [opening up of the] hearts of the children of men" (D&C 64:22).

And "remember that on this, the Lord's day, thou shalt offer thine oblations [sacrificial gifts] and thy sacraments unto the Most High, confessing thy sins unto thy brethren, and before the Lord" (D&C 59:12).

More than any of us, he can keep confidences. As he purges us he promises he will remember no more our transgressions (see D&C 58:42). Even when they are committed against him and his mission of mercy.

WHEN ARE WE ACCEPTABLE?

If we have misgivings and self-doubts as we approach sacred ordinances, a judgment day in advance of the judgment day has been provided for us. He has given us a clear signal on what he expects of us: "Verily I say unto you, all among them who know their hearts are honest, and are broken, and their spirits contrite, and are willing to observe their covenants by sacrifice—yea, every sacrifice which I, the Lord, shall command—they are accepted of me" (D&C 97:8).

Here again willingness and desires for righteousness commend us to heaven, as well as all our acts and dispositions toward righteousness. It appears that willingness combined with covenant-making equals worthiness (we covenant that we are willing).

But what of "all who *know* their hearts are honest"? Can we trust ourselves to know ourselves? Do we know whether our hearts are honest? With his help, yes. For he "is a discerner of the thoughts and intents of the heart" (Hebrews 4:12; D&C 33:1).

THE CENTER PLACE

When the first group of clustering saints reached the "center place" of Zion—Jackson County, Missouri—Joseph taught them that it was the veritable center of the continent, "equidistant from Atlantic and Pacific Oceans." He then "afforded a glimpse of the future": The place to be designated Zion was also the locus of the New Jerusalem. The people caught the vision.

Joseph prayed that the Lord would "beautify the place of His sanctuary," and that "He may make the place of his feet glorious" and "where the feast of fat things will be given to the just."[1] The "feast of fat things" was to follow the dedication of both the land and the temple site.

Now the uppermost concern was whether this band of neophyte saints would fully dedicate themselves to Christ. It was a time and place for their covenant-renewal.

Just prior to celebrating their first Sabbath there, a revelation was given. The verses reenthrone commandments given to the ancient children of Israel. Joseph, a man like unto Moses, came down, as it were, from communion with God and brought divine instruction as if written in stone. The decalogue is reestablished with two added ones: "Thank the Lord thy God in all things," and "offer a sacrifice . . . of a broken heart and a contrite spirit." All this is to keep oneself "unspotted from the [vices of] the world" (D&C 59:7–9).

In this spirit the saints approached the sacrament. Divine counsel was later expanded and clarified: "Get close to the Lord. . . . spirits drawn out to God and His Son. . . . Hearts humble, contrite and at peace . . . soften hearts of the participants and draw them near to God, perfect love and harmony."[2]

---

1. Smith, *History of the Church,* 1:196–98.
2. Cited in Quinn, "Prayer Circles," 104.

BABETTE AND THE LOVE FEAST

A legend still lives in Denmark, the tale of Babette's feast.

In a minister's home where she has sought refuge from war in Paris, Babette joins two sisters. One day she suddenly learns she has won a prize of 10,000 francs. She spends all of her prize to purchase the makings of one superb feast in the little village. No one knows she is a culinary genius.

While others wait on table, she remains in the kitchen in her apron and, as she brings it all together, her joy is in doing what she does best, from turtle soup to the succulent grapes for dessert.

The group savors the meal. Then spiritual powers assert themselves. Men and women who have been guilty of petty estrangements begin impulsively to rejoice in mutual forgiveness. Fellow feeling abounds. All become reconciled and bonded.

Then, in a gesture and a toast, the most prominent guest—a general who has known disillusion and cynicism—arises. He discourses on the glories of divine mercy. Unaware she is only a few steps away, he begins to reminisce about a woman chef in Paris. She could, he says, "transform a dinner into a kind of love affair, an affair that made no distinction between bodily appetite and spiritual appetite."

Afterward, when her two sisters realize the immense cost and sacrifice, they cry out, "You should not have given all that you owned for us." She replies quietly, "An artist is never poor." Then, anticipating the glories of the hereafter, her sisters embrace her and say, "Ah, how you will delight the angels."

This is the spirit of feasting in the name of the Lord.

CLAY IN THE HANDS OF THE POTTER

We have watched a potter at work in Hebron. He sits at a table-wheel. Supple clay, the best-textured clay, is at the center. With bare and calloused feet he rotates the wheel at a slow, consistent rate. He applies water in an exact amount with expertise gained father-to-son. He holds his hands like the edge of a lathe. Slowly a pitcher or a cup or a vase emerges. If all goes well, he then seals and glazes it to a beautiful sheen.

But if the clay hardens prematurely, it becomes resistant and unusable. It has to be shattered and "thrown back." Then the process begins over.

He who has in mind a masterpiece has to have the right hands for it. And the skills. And workable clay.

We are told that the proper pathway to Christ is "a broken heart and a contrite spirit" (3 Nephi 9:20). In Hebrew, contrite is *nakeh,* meaning smitten. A related word, *dakah,* means to be crumbled, to be bruised, to be broken into pieces. Still another means to be buffeted as by a wave.

In a lifetime, however drastic they sound, these words apply to most of us.

The Master of masters is a molder. And he can reach beyond the surface to "wrench our very heart strings."[1] Those who become like clay in the hands of the Potter will emerge in prime condition as not only servants but friends; not only friends but sons and daughters in whom he confides.

Heber C. Kimball, himself a potter, spoke in these terms at the home of the Prophet. Joseph arose. He commended this virtue of humility and pliability. He then referred to Jesus's parable of the vine and the branches, saying, "if we keep the commandments of God we should bring forth fruit and be the friends of God, and know what our Lord did."[2]

---

1. See John Taylor citing the Prophet Joseph in *Journal of Discourses,* 24:197.
2. Smith, *History of the Church,* 4:478.

WOUNDS HEALED, EVEN ERASED

Elder Melvin J. Ballard taught:

> We do things for which we are sorry and desire to be forgiven, or we have erred against someone and given injury. If there is a feeling in our hearts that we are sorry for what we have done, if there is a feeling in our souls that we would like to be forgiven, then the method to obtain forgiveness is not through rebaptism; it is not to make confession to man, but it is to repent of our sins, to go to those against whom we have sinned or transgressed and obtain their forgiveness, and then repair to the sacrament table where, if we have sincerely repented and put ourselves in proper condition, we shall be forgiven, and spiritual healing will come to our souls.

It will really enter into our being.

You have felt it.

✳ I am a witness that there is a spirit attending the administration of the sacrament that warms the soul from head to foot; you feel the wounds of the spirit being healed and the load being lifted. Comfort and happiness come to the soul that is worthy and truly desirous of partaking of this spiritual food.

> Why do we not all come? Why do we not come regularly to the sacrament service and partake of these emblems and perform this highest worship we can give to our Father in the name of his Beloved Son? Is it because we do not appreciate it? Is it because we do not feel the necessity for this blessing, or is it because, perhaps, we feel ourselves unworthy to partake of these emblems?[1]

---

1. Ballard, *Sermons and Missionary Services*, 149.

CONTACT AND COMMUNION

We learn from President David O. McKay:

No more sacred ordinance is administered in the Church of Christ than the administration of the sacrament. . . .

There are three things fundamentally important associated with the administration of the sacrament. The first is self-discernment. It is introspection. "This do in remembrance of me," but we should partake worthily, each one examining himself with respect to his worthiness.

Secondly, there is a covenant made; a covenant even more than a promise. . . .

Thirdly, there is another blessing, and that is a sense of close relationship with the Lord. There is an opportunity to commune with oneself and to commune with the Lord. . . .

We recommend that we surround this sacred ordinance with more reverence, with perfect order, that each one who comes to the house of God may meditate upon his goodness and silently and prayerfully express appreciation for God's goodness. Let the sacrament hour be one experience of the day in which the worshiper tries at least to realize within himself that it is possible for him to commune with his God.

Great events have happened in this Church because of such communion, because of the responsiveness of the soul to the inspiration of the Almighty. I know it is real. . . .

But the lesson I wish to leave tonight is: Let us make that sacrament hour one of the most impressive means of coming in contact with God's Spirit. Let the Holy Ghost, to which we are entitled, lead us into his presence, and may we sense that nearness, and have a prayer offered in our hearts which he will hear.[1]

---

1. In Conference Report, April 1946, 112, 114, 116.

FACE TOWARD HIM

Found in the papers of a father who, as a single parent, raised three boys:

> I was awakened the other morning about 4 o'clock in my room by a little voice just beside my bed in the dark asking for a drink. I got the little lad a drink, and he lay quiet for a moment and then asked, "Father, may I sing myself to sleep?" And I said, "Yes, dear, go ahead." But soon he got up so much enthusiasm that I told him he had better stop, or none of the rest of us could sleep. Then he was quiet awhile, but soon I heard his little voice again in the perfect stillness of the night. "Father, have you got your face turned toward me?" I said, "Yes, little boy," and the darkness was as the light of day to him.

So we can understand the invitation of the Master to "seek the face of the Lord always, that in patience ye may possess your souls" (D&C 101:38).

What is the connection between seeking his face and patience? How do we "possess our souls"?

Luke has it. In Greek the sentence means "in constancy ye may possess your souls," or again, in "faithful endurance ye may possess your souls." Or "in patient consistency," which includes waiting and preparing.

To this condition Jesus attaches some of his greatest promises of unfolding his face—"It shall be in his own time, and in his own way, and according to his own will" (D&C 88:68).

The Lord has his own due time. But as President Hugh B. Brown once said, "I have never quite been able to synchronize my watch with his timetable."

We learn that when we seek to turn to "the joy and light of the Lord's countenance" we can see everything better (see D&C 88:52–58).

Presently we may be two-faced or three-faced. But his face is one of constant and steady watchcare.

A TIME TO TRUST THE SILENCE

"Sometimes during solitude I hear truth spoken with clarity and freshness; uncolored and untranslated it speaks from within myself in a language original but inarticulate, heard only with the soul, and I realize I brought it with me, was never taught it nor can I effectively teach it to another."[1]

We have often sat in small circles with students who have come to Jerusalem and asked them, "What is your high moment so far?"

Frequently they answer: "Partaking of the sacrament in the upper room." The "upper room" is their renaming of the Assembly Room—three stories and three sides of glass inside stone arches, the perfect frame for the golden city and the mountain of the Lord.

Within that vista Jesus lived the last week of his life.

Many report a feeling of familiarity at these sites or sights in the Holy Land. "It is as if I've been here before"—somehow born to it, somehow lodged in their deeper selves, intimations from within, yet from afar.

Otherwise they cannot account for the impact of reliving "on location" the lives of the worthy men and women of earlier days—and of the Christ.

Teachers learn to stay out of the way and provide students solitude and moments of silence. Moments sometimes become hours and last into the night.

"Be still and know that I am God" (D&C 101:16).

"Then shall ye know that ye have seen me, that I am, and that I am the true light that is in you, and that you are in me; otherwise ye could not abound" (D&C 88:50).

---

1. Hugh B. Brown, *Eternal Quest*, 435.

CHILDREN AS THE GREATEST

We were in a refugee camp. Children gathered near hovels, battered by swirling, powderlike dust. Visitors handed small comforts out to stretched-up hands—a toothbrush, a pen, a bit of candy.

One little boy went to a cupboard, climbed inside, and closed the doors surrounded by darkness. "When does he come out?" someone asked. "He only comes out at mealtime."

Children are needy. In the absence of genuine care, children tend to withdraw into cupboards and into themselves. But they still want to find and give love—as the note thrown over the wall of an orphanage reads: "Whoever finds this, I love you."

A teacher I know has worked all her mature life with children who were crippled, challenged, slow learning, and disadvantaged. She reports that this paragraph validates her observations of children:

> What did the Master recommend?—These strange sentences about "becoming as a little child"? Are the virtues of the childlike more obvious than the vices of the childish?
>
> Maybe he was saying more, saying that we are not, as empiricists assert, born an empty tablet on which the chalk of childhood writes. Maybe he was saying that a child has swift, untinctured affinity and response to his own burning deeps. He is exemplary not, as is so often said, in vulnerable readiness to believe others' voices, but in soul-unity that prevents disbelief of his own. He has a whole, happy, healthy relationship with the core of creativity and spirituality which is his glory-laden spirit.[1]

Jesus at Jericho said something just as stupendous. Children are acceptable. Children are admirable. In the esteem of heaven they are among the great. He answered disciples who were vying, prodded by their mother, for a future position near the very throne of God (and apparently were still clamoring even during the Last Supper). Jesus said that children, and those like them, are to be the *very greatest* in the kingdom of heaven.

---

1. Truman G. Madsen, *Eternal Man,* 77.

THE CHILDISH AND CHILDLIKE

For those of us who are grown-up, mature, and worldly wise—we who have put away our childhood—what, after all, is so venerable in a child?

Jesus's teaching offers some clues that come down through the centuries.

A child is full of wonder. With wide eyes and open lips he is in frequent awe of his world. He still has the unspoiled capacity to marvel at what we think are ordinary things.

A child does not pretend that he is self-sufficient. He cries and cries out his needs. And he can be taught.

Typically, a child needs no special reason nor season to be happy. He just is happy.

A child heals quickly from wounds of head and of heart. And before he learns to pronounce words, he responds to the nurture of lingering hugs.

A child forgives. He easily feels his way beyond the failings of those who care. As a wrinkled great-grandmother said of her visiting little one, "She doesn't know I'm old. She just loves me."

A child is all inborn sympathy. Embracing the contagion of sorrow or gladness, he matches others tear for tear, or dances with glee needing no explanation.

Among the ancients it was said a holy person reaches his prime, whatever his age or status of learning and wisdom, when he prays and loves like a little child.[1]

In sum, a child embodies what Isaiah envisioned the glorious Redeemer-figure would be: In his very childlikeness he was, and is, "Wonderful, Counsellor" (Isaiah 9:6).

---

1. Buber, *Tales of the Hasidim,* 139.

PRAY ALWAYS?

Ten times in modern scripture we are admonished to "pray always" (D&C 10:5; 19:38; 20:33; 31:12; 61:39; 88:126; 90:24; 93:49, 50; 101:81).

We are also admonished to offer up our vows and oblations "on all days and at all times" (D&C 59:11). And to seal our best resolves with covenant.

The Lord adds: "Ye must practice virtue and holiness before me continually" (D&C 46:33). And "Look unto me in every thought" (D&C 6:36).

This is intensified on the Sabbath.

Brigham Young advises:

> I do not know any other way for the Latter-day Saints than for every breath to be virtually a prayer for God to guide and direct his people, and that he will never suffer us to possess anything that will be an injury to us. I am satisfied that this should be the feeling of every Latter-day Saint in the world. If you are making a bargain, if you are talking in the house, visiting in the social party, going forth in the dance, every breath should virtually be a prayer that God will preserve us from sin and from the effects of sin.
>
> Let us be humble, fervent, submissive, yielding ourselves to the will of the Lord, and there is no danger but that we shall have his Spirit to guide us. If we will open our lips and call upon our Heavenly Father, in the name of Jesus, we will have the spirit of prayer.
>
> I have proved this to be the best way. If we do everything in the season thereof, attending to our prayers and daily labors in their proper order and at the right time, all will go well.[1]

---

1. In *Journal of Discourses*, 13:155.

INVINCIBLE INGRATITUDE

At the top of a steep hill a man was cutting his lawn. In the corner of his eye he saw a lad facing down the sidewalk on a wagon. The next time he looked with horror. The lad was hurtling downward, oblivious to the death-dealing freeway below.

The man raced toward the wagon, then realized he could only catch it by a desperate leap. One hand caught on, but then he was dragged and scraped. The wagon finally stopped. The lad turned to his bleeding and bruised benefactor. "Hey, mister, get your hands off my wagon!"

"For what doth it profit a man if a gift is bestowed upon him, and he receive not the gift? Behold, he rejoices not in that which is given unto him, neither rejoices in him who is the giver of the gift" (D&C 88:33).

We can enjoy only that which we are willing to receive.

Christ has been and is involved in our lives, and he has made diving leaps in our behalf. We may be asleep to him, indifferent to him, even callously opposed to him. But he has promised that those who receive him will receive more abundantly, "even power" (D&C 71:6). He has promised that this abundance will be multiplied through the manifestations of his Spirit (see D&C 70:13).

"For whosoever hath, to him shall be given, and he shall have more abundance: but whosoever hath not, from him shall be taken away even that he hath" (Matthew 13:12).

"The great misery of departed spirits in the world of spirits, where they go after death, is to know that they come short of the glory that others enjoy and that they might have enjoyed themselves, and they are their own accusers."[1]

---

1. Smith, *History of the Church,* 5:425.

GIVING THANKS IN THE SPIRIT

A year and a half after the Church was organized, there was a renewing upon the saints of the Ten Commandments. To the command "thou shalt love the Lord thy God" is appended, "and in the name of Jesus Christ thou shalt serve him" (D&C 59:5).

This Sabbath revelation adds an eleventh commandment: "Thou shalt thank the Lord thy God in all things" (D&C 59:7). As if fervent giving of thanks is vital to Sabbath observance. As if the high expectations of "offering up of [our] most holy desires" (D&C 95:16) are blunted unless we express soulful gratitude. As if one holy desire is to express uninhibited thank-yous.

Earlier, in March 1831 at Kirtland, the people had been admonished: "Ye must give thanks unto God in the Spirit for whatsoever blessing ye are blessed with" (D&C 46:32). Six months later the plea was made again, this time with promise: "He who receiveth all things [even all things daunting and trying?] with thankfulness shall be made glorious" (D&C 78:19).

All this means give thanks unto God while the Spirit is still upon us. It means give thanks unto God and his Son who are in touch through the sacrament. And it means thanksgiving amidst his giving, especially when we stand in holy places (see D&C 101:22, 64, 67).

"WITH MORE REVERENCE, WITH PERFECT ORDER"

President David O. McKay with his brethren issued this statement:

We [the First Presidency] recommend that we surround this sacred ordinance with more reverence, with perfect order, that each one who comes to the house of God may meditate upon his goodness and silently and prayerfully express appreciation for God's goodness. Let the sacrament hour be one experience of the day in which the worshiper tries at least to realize within himself that it is possible for him to commune with his God.

Great events have happened in this Church because of such communion, because of the responsiveness of the soul to the inspiration of the Almighty. I know it is real. . . .

Let us make that sacrament hour one of the most impressive means of coming in contact with God's Spirit. Let the Holy Ghost, to which we are entitled, lead us into his presence, and may we sense that nearness, and have a prayer offered in our hearts which he will hear.[1]

This is the man who taught that reverence is "the most sublime attribute of the human soul." Because, I take it, it melds together everything Christlike: gratitude, respect, honor, proper dependence, and openness to the will of the Lord.

---

1. David O. McKay, in Conference Report, April 1946, 112, 114, 116.

"LET THE TABLES TURN
ON YOUR SERVING"

Author Heather Moore writes, "One statement changed my outlook forever on the administration of the sacrament and the priesthood power behind the weekly ordinance." She then excerpts a talk on "The Savior, the Sacrament, and Self-Worth":

> You faithful sisters, married or unmarried, who move daily (and hardly with a break) from the garden plot to the crucial minutia of food labels to the cups and measures of cookery;
>
> You who struggle and preside in the kitchen and keep vigil;
>
> You who reach out to the perennial needs of your family and loved ones;
>
> You who with artistry gather flowers and turn an ordinary table into an altar that summons prayer and thanksgiving;
>
> You who by your very presence turn eating into a feast—into dining in the name of the Lord—and who, therefore, bring a bountiful measure of grace to your table;
>
> Lend your faith to boys and sometimes inept men who officiate at the sacrament table.
>
> Let the tables turn on your serving. Lend your faith to our trying to act as you do in Christlike dignity, [for this is as close as we may ever come to your divine calling to give and to nurture life itself] . . .
>
> Come to a foretaste of the marriage supper of the Lamb.

Her conclusion? "The priesthood is an offering for everyone."[1]

---

1. Moore, in *Desert Saints,* 379, citing Madsen, "The Savior, the Sacrament, and Self-Worth."

HE WAS KNOWN IN THE
BREAKING OF BREAD

At a time when some among the saints were perverse and foolish, the Master asked, "Canst thou run about longer as a blind guide? Or canst thou be humble and meek, and conduct yourself wisely before me?" (D&C 19:40–41).

If there are blinding scales on our eyes, how can they be removed?

Perhaps we are being taught how in the incident of the two disciples on the road to Emmaus. They fall in with a stranger. They undertake a journey of many miles and begin to talk.

They speak of things that have just occurred in the big city. "You have not heard of the stir made by a Nazarene? A man put to death during the Passover feast?" He returns the compliment: "Have you not heard the sayings of the prophets?" He begins to expound them.

At first they are "slow of heart" to believe what the prophets have spoken. What would it be like? To have the scriptures "given, even as they are in mine own bosom, to the salvation of mine own elect" (D&C 35:20). That's how they were given that day.

Later, as they sit at table, perhaps as he reaches for the bread or the cup, the sleeves of his robe pull back. Did they then see the scars in his wrists or hands? The record says, "He was known . . . in breaking of bread" (Luke 24:35).

That moment of recognition and re-cognition may come to all of us as we partake of his sacrament. Afterward we may well ask, "Did not our heart[s] burn within us, while he talked with us by the way, and while he opened to us the scriptures?" (Luke 24:32)

REPENTANCE AND FORGETTING

Repentance is not, in our weak and double-minded moments, as we fervently wish—it is not just a matter of forgetting. "If only I could wipe out the memory . . . I would be free."

Not so. If one takes poison, he may receive forgiveness from everyone, even himself. But the poison is still there, still festering. It requires an antidote. The longer we wait, and the longer we continue the intake, the more desperate our condition.

We know, from the scriptures, that one day we will have "a bright recollection of all our guilt" (Alma 11:43). We will remember all that we have forgotten, including all that we have worked hard to forget. In the language of a shrewd observer: "'I did that,' says my memory. 'I could not have done that,' says my conscience. Eventually the memory yields."

He will read our hearts—every trace recorded of the long, hard journey—with abiding understanding. He knows our sins accurately and intimately. He wrote them on his own inner world in Gethsemane. He willingly exposed himself to the identical feelings of abandonment, guilt, and darkness.

Yet he mastered them because he gave no heed to the temptations that have lured us and mired us and become monkeys on our back.

But if we have repented through Christ and been purged through his power, the future memory flood will not be bitter or tormenting. It will instead be a welter of gratitude for healed sores, for the pain that is gone, for the relief that has replaced our divided and mud-spattered and guilty self.

This is full-scale remembering with peace, with gratitude, with joy. Otherwise, as the Prophet Joseph put it, "We always have that wrong gnawing us."[1]

---

1. *Words of Joseph Smith*, 369.

Sabbath

MEET TOGETHER OFT

Jesus commands his disciples to "meet together"—and to meet together "oft" (D&C 20:55, 75).

We inherit the promise that when we gather together "as touching one thing"—that is, unitedly—he will attend us. He will be present (D&C 6:32; see also D&C 27:18; 42:3).

This was a promise he himself kept.

We read from the record: "Therefore, I would that ye should behold [more than hear] that the Lord truly did teach the [Nephite] people, for the space of three days; *and after that he did show himself unto them oft,* and did break bread *oft,* and bless it, and give it unto them" (3 Nephi 26:13).

His Spirit attends his saints as promised while they are together. "I am in your midst and ye cannot see me" (D&C 38:7).

These Nephite people had attained great spiritual heights. In fact, Jesus said that he had not found so great faith in his home country, the land of holiness (see 3 Nephi 19:35–36). Yet they remained in need of him.

What they aspired to, all of us—the best of us and the worst of us—can do: to meet each other every seven days. We then invite and invoke him at the center and also at the ragged edge of our lives.

Rarely in his ordinances is there a "once and for all." We need renewing. And we need it often.

FROM A YOU TO A THOU

Sometimes when we are called to give blessings we invoke "thou" language. We speak to the person as a "thou" instead of the daily usage of "you." We are newly aware of what we too often forget—that in the eyes of God we are holy personages. Not a mere "it" or a mere "you." Something about us is holy.

So, when proclaiming the Sabbath as celebration, modern revelation moves into "thou" language: "For verily this is a day appointed unto you to rest from your labors, and to pay thy devotions unto the Most High" (D&C 59:10). Here in mid-sentence one is lifted beyond a "you" to a "thou." The usage continues:

- *Thy* food (to be prepared with singleness of heart).
- *Thou* shalt do none other thing.
- *Thy* fasting may be perfect (for fasting is rejoicing and prayer).
- *Thy* joy may be full.

This may reflect an ancient saying that on the Sabbath you are at your best. More—during this day you are, as it were, another self. A better spirit has taken possession of you. So the wife may smile at the dinner table and say to her husband or children, "You are not yourself today. And it is an improvement."

THE SABBATH AS PARADISIACAL GLORY

"Blessed are the meek: for they shall inherit the earth" (Matthew 5:5; 3 Nephi 12:5). In Greek this more precisely means "inherit the land." Consecrated people will inherit consecrated land. But shouldn't we inherit something better?

The Prophet Joseph makes clear that once the earth reaches its glorified state, there will not be in the whole universe anything better.

The classical idea that heaven is utterly beyond our view, beyond space and time, beyond all elemental, mundane reality; and the dogma that humankind will finally transcend flesh and become pure mind involved in pure contemplation of ethereal light, is, for many, enchanting. But it is misleading.

The power of purity will extend to everything. The earth is not a launching pad from which we aspire to fly, to escape and never return. It is not destined to become so much cosmic and inferior refuse.

Instead, the resurrection of the earth and of the human family is resurrection of element. "Spirit and element, inseparably connected" (D&C 93:33) in man will be exactly duplicated in the earth and the cosmos. Abraham was taught that the earth will resume a position in the cosmos "nigh unto Kolob" (Abraham 3:9). It will be "rolled back into the presence of God and crowned with Celestial Glory."[1]

Hence, the Sabbath-earth itself will define sacred space. It will rotate in its times and seasons in sacred time—the Millennium. Participants upon it will live together in the spirit of jubilee. Nature will return to its sweetest fragrance, glorified beyond our present capacities to fully grasp.

The Lord walks on the crest of heaven seeking to help us make a heaven on earth—because in the long run he means to make not a heaven beyond earth, but a heaven of earth. To inherit it is the highest spirituality we—or anyone—can reach.

---

1. Discourse, January 5, 1841, Nauvoo, Illinois, in William Clayton's Private Book; Church History Library, 275.

SABBATH AS QUEEN

We have visited Safed, the high-altitude village in the Holy Land, and breathed the clean, vigorous mountain air and seen the remnants of an earlier golden era. This is like the "city . . . set on an hill" that Jesus referred to (Matthew 5:14).

We have walked to the perpetual spring where, prior to Sabbath Eve, observant Jews plunge into bracing, near-freezing water and don clean clothing for the Sabbath.

Our guides point in different directions and tell us that one of the great rabbis (Luria) established a greeting procedure for Friday afternoons as the Sabbath approached. He walked into the fields singing (as now in almost every synagogue worldwide): "Come, queen Sabbath."

It is the queen mother in orthodox homes who lights the candles, pulling her hands toward her eyes as if to beckon the light.

Jesus's teaching in the New Testament is rich in just such royal wedding imagery (see Revelation 19:7). He teaches that the Sabbath which is made for man and for woman is meaningful to God himself.

His parables hint of a king who has made a bridal chamber, plastered it, painted it, and adorned it. Now what does the chamber lack? Obviously a bride.

After the days of creation, what did the universe still lack? The Sabbath.

So the Sabbath is a bride. Its celebration is like a wedding, and the bride is to come lovely and bedecked and perfumed.

How do we view the Sabbath?

SABBATH ON THE PLAINS

Before the saints left Nauvoo, the promise was given, "If you observe strictly the Sabbath you shall be protected, but you must serve the Lord." So except in emergency situations, the wagon companies halted on each Sabbath, wary and often weary. They sang hymns, held sacrament services, taught and testified, prayed.

Brigham's first contingent of emigrants included many young striplings. The mobocracy was behind then, but they were unfamiliar with plains hazards. Soon ordinary restraints were let down. Frivolity followed—games like "arrests" and mock trials—boys "found guilty," tied to log chains, dragged around the camp amidst a noisy parade of tin pans, lids, kettles. Adults too lapsed into swearing and murmuring.

(Wilford Woodruff said it reminded him of the loss of identity of Zion's Camp, which led to cholera and some deaths. He didn't want to see more of it.)

Brother Brigham called a halt and gathered them all together. This, the first Sabbath on the plains, was set apart as a day of fasting and prayer. The company camped near a stream, bathed, put on clean clothing, shaved, and prepared for the Sabbath.

On the Sabbath they gathered in a secluded place, knelt in the grass, and offered prayer. The Spirit of God was poured out upon them. Mockery and undue levity ceased.

ON GLADNESS ON THE SABBATH

"There is nothing in the religion that Christ has restored to the earth in this dispensation that requires any soul to go about with a sorrowful countenance and a downcast mien. There is nothing in it to make us uncheerful or unhappy; but, to the contrary, there is everything in it calculated to make us cheerful in our hearts and joyful and peaceful in our souls."[1]

"We do not, however, wish to observe the Sabbath after the puritanical order. God does not desire to bring us into bondage. He has not told us that we may not smile on the Sabbath day, nor even laugh, if there is something to laugh at. It is proper to sing, if we sing proper songs. If there are any songs that might not be termed spiritual exactly, if they are pure and contain good sentiment, and are enlightening to the mind and enlivening to the heart, they are all right.

"There is a time and place for everything. In our meetings of worship we should join in the hymn, in the psalm, and in the spiritual song, as well as in the prayer and partake of the sacrament, and rejoice before the Lord. And we should not do this with a mournful countenance, but with a joyful heart and a glad countenance; for God delights in this. This idea of mourning and sorrow, and a long face, as a part of religion, is all wrong. It never was a part of the religion of Jesus Christ, but is an invention of man."[2]

---

1. Joseph F. Smith, in Stuy, *Collected Discourses,* Vol. 3: July 16, 1893.
2. Charles W. Penrose, in Stuy, *Collected Discourses,* Vol. 3: June 25, 1893.

IS THE SABBATH AN IMPEDIMENT?

For some of us the Sabbath is an unwelcome red light. It impedes the flow of our strivings. It interrupts and brings to a halt activities we care about. It muffles our cherished enjoyments.

But that is exactly backward. The Sabbath is to be the merited destination—the fulfillment of a week of toil. It is the pot of gold at the end of the rainbow, the earned celebration of labor and work well done or at least done. It is not the interruption of life. It is a weekly pleasant culmination of life.

For us it can be a sanctuary in time—closing out the conflicts and competitions outside. It is "time out."

And it is time in and time for what we have postponed or neglected spiritually: "That thy joy may be full" (D&C 59:13).

It can be a time for hibernation from chaos and chores and keeping ahead of the encroachments of dust and dirt. It can be dress-up time. It can be "now I can relax and relish" time.

We are so geared to flurry and hurry, so intent on getting things done. From youth up we need to learn, whatever else we do on the Sabbath, to savor and in so doing sanctify the day.

It is said that when it is properly observed, the very texture of the Sabbath changes. It is like a meteorological shift—as if the elements and the trees and the flowers put on a happy face. "Nature breathes her sweetest fragrance on the holy Sabbath day."[1]

We distinguish work and play. We also distinguish work and rest. We need to distinguish work and feast. For in the mode of Sabbath celebration, every thing is a feast.

---

1. "Come Away to the Sunday School," *Hymns*, no. 276.

SABBATH AS BANQUET

Much of our legacy defines the Sabbath as a banquet.

When Moses led the children of Israel in the wilderness, a double portion of manna was given just before the Sabbath, but none on the Sabbath. The day was recognizable in two ways—by what was absent and what was present.

Jews serve the most beautiful meal of the week on Shabbat Eve. The mother often prepares for as much as two days before, and one of the traditional dishes is a kind of stew that simmers all night long after sundown and then needs only to be served.

The table process is itself a form of ritual, and it requires traditional preparations and special songs and readings. It is, to quote one writer, "a sanctuary in time."

Something of the same spirit attends America's Thanksgiving dinner.

It customarily involves the bringing in of the stranger. "Come and share our Shabbat." It is a feast even for the poorest man in the poorest ghetto. Why? Because even if he cannot afford the twisted loaves and the meat and the fish, the people in that area will see that he has them. It is a requirement. So on that special day, even a poor man or woman is rich.

SABBATH AND FINISHING

The earliest texts on the creation narrative say, "On the seventh day—the Sabbath—God finished his work." That is sometimes interpreted as "completed his work."

But completing is an activity. And do we not read that God "rested" from his labors?

It is suggested that God did "finish his work" on the Sabbath by one act of creation. He created "*menuhah*," which is tranquillity. Surely that is what *we* should seek to create on the Sabbath

But there is more about Sabbath completion. The key verses are as follows (this is Joseph Smith's commentary on chapter 8 of Revelation):

> We are to understand that as God made the world in six days, and on the seventh day he finished his work, and sanctified it, and also formed man out of the dust of the earth, even so, in the beginning of the seventh thousand years will the Lord God sanctify the earth, and complete the salvation of man, and judge all things, and shall redeem all things, except that which he hath not put into his power, when he shall have sealed all things, unto the end of all things (D&C 77:12).

This means that when a resplendent earth was prepared, the highest priority was for Adam and Eve to be introduced into the Garden. And this was the seventh day.

We may fulfill the spirit of these preeminent events on our own pre-Millennial weekly Sabbaths. We are to call on the Lord God to sanctify *us*, re-forming and transforming us "unto the end of all things."

Music That Ascends

SINGING TO PERFECTION

We walked one day into St. Anne's, built near the pool of Bethesda in east Jerusalem. It is an unadorned chapel—clean white stone walls, high-vaulted ceilings, and massive pillars. Its stature is remarkable. Its acoustics are stunning. If you stand close to the entryway and sing a few notes, six or seven reverberations follow.

We were there with an untrained lyrical soprano, who sang "by ear." She looked upward and began to sing "I Know That My Redeemer Lives." Echoes resounded and fused many notes, like the sonorities of antiphonal organs.

Standing nearby was a renowned concert pianist. He had composed and arranged many a hymn and performed worldwide a repertoire from Mozart to Aaron Copland.

"That crowns all my musical experiences," he said, adding, "It was more than her technique."

We tried to define why we sensed the "more":

- Because we felt that the song ascended to heaven and that heaven sang back. It seemed to open up another world of rapturous feelings.
- Because it reached to and unlocked the unutterable within us. "The Spirit itself maketh intercession with our spirits with striving that cannot be expressed" (JST, Romans 8:26).
- Because her song became worship. And worship is defined in modern revelation as two-way, "grace for grace"—our grace reaching up in supportive love. And divine powers, the powers of godliness, flowing down.

So, mightily, song can be prayer and prayer can be song, and both will be answered.

CELESTIAL LYRICS

Imagine you are looking over the shoulder of a gifted organist. Sheet music is before you. At the top is written, "Lyrics by Jesus the Christ. Music yet to be revealed."

In the future, we are promised that "all shall know me, who remain, even from the least unto the greatest, and shall be filled with the knowledge of the Lord, and shall see eye to eye, and shall lift up their voice,[1] and with the voice together sing this new song, saying:"

The Lord hath brought again Zion; The Lord hath redeemed his people, Israel, According to the election of grace, Which was brought to pass by the faith And covenant of their fathers.
The Lord hath redeemed his people;
And Satan is bound and time is no longer.
The Lord hath gathered all things in one.
The Lord hath brought down Zion from above.
The Lord hath brought up Zion from beneath.
The earth hath travailed and brought forth her strength;
And truth is established in her bowels;
And the heavens have smiled upon her;
And she is clothed with the glory of her God;
For he stands in the midst of his people.
Glory, and honor, and power, and might,
Be ascribed to our God; for he is full of mercy,
Justice, grace and truth, and peace,
Forever and ever, Amen. (D&C 84:98–102)

We sing, and we shout, and sometimes we whistle in the dark. We hum half-remembered words, or beat rhythms with foot or fingers. Sometimes we join in memory-enriched hymns.

But this will be the "Song of Songs."

---

1. It does not say "their *voices,*" (plural) but their *voice.* We will sing as one.

SINGING THE NEW SONG

It is called the "new song"—to be sung at a time to come, at a family reunion that will be the mother of all reunions. Psalm 98 cries "Sing unto the Lord a new song," the song of redeeming love.

It will be sung in new-old language. Perhaps it will be "the tongue of angels," perhaps the language of Eden, which was the language of paradise. Or the language of all creatures above before they came below.

But can this majestic melody be known to mere mortals?

What if at that hour our memory veil is thinned or drawn aside? What if we are given back the words and music of former and higher spheres? What if those halt of tongue and feeble of voice are given a new surge and can speak and sing in full attunement? What if labored rehearsals and rhythmic batons are replaced by a wave of the Spirit that at once synchronizes and melds voice and instrument into one voice?

Then, as Parley P. Pratt envisioned it, we can: "Move with grace immortal to the soul-inspiring measure of music flowing from a thousand instruments, blend in harmonious numbers, with celestial voices, in heavenly song, or mingle in graceful circles with joyous thousands, immersed in the same spirit, and move in unison and harmony of motion, as if one heart, one pulse, one thrill of heavenly melody inspired the whole."[1]

We may suppose that our fervent song-prayers are only heard from afar. But that distance will be closed. For there are hints that as he has joined in all the stages of our spiritual perfecting, the Host among the heavenly hosts will join us in this triumphal song to the glory of the Father.

---

1. Pratt, *Key to the Science of Theology,* 162.

SINGING ACROSS THE WATERS

Out of a long tradition the Hebrew language not only permits but enjoins verve in singing.

The words for song include *zmra* and *zilpah* (*zimair* is a gazelle that lightly touches the ground, hinting of melody or psalm), rooted in the idea of striking with fingers, suggesting string instruments. Related words connote celebrating, giving praise, singing forth.

Our own book of Ether details a prolonged and perilous journey on the punishing, turbulent sea. The voyagers were in watertight, double-dish-like barges. Pounding waves often submerged them, and they worked their way to the surface. Air, food, water, and wind were crucial.

The voyage lasted 322 days!

Prior to launch, the brother of Jared had been abruptly chastised. Three and a half years had slipped by without his praying. Or, perhaps, he had prayed without real intent. Now, however, we read that he prayed and sang daily, even all-daily.

"And they did sing praises unto the Lord" in the midst of winds which "did never cease to blow," with hearts which did never cease to sing. "Yea, the brother of Jared did sing praises unto the Lord, and he did thank and praise the Lord all the day long; and when the night came, they did not cease to praise the Lord" (Ether 6:8–9).

Surely voices singing even in low volume would become hoarse and then silent in so prolonged a chorus. Unless they were like the concourses of angels in Lehi's vision. They were not always vocalizing but were "*in the attitude* of singing and praising their God" (1 Nephi 1:8).

It might be said that these venturing pilgrims prayed to God with such fervor because they realized their very lives depended on it.

So do ours.

LOVE SO AMAZING

Some time ago, the Tabernacle Choir performed in Jerusalem within the sequestered area known as the Garden Tomb. For nearly three hours that sacred place was reserved for them to make a video recording.

In that impressive setting the choir rehearsed and sang the moving anthem "When I Survey the Wondrous Cross," sometimes called "Love So Amazing." The song's final stanzas are these:

See from his head, his hands, his feet,
Sorrow and blood flow mingled down!
Did e'er such love and sorrow meet,
Or thorns compose so rich a crown!

Were the whole realm of nature mine,
That were a present far too small;
Love so amazing, so divine,
Demands my soul, my life, my all!

Perhaps the choir did not need the visual aid. Perhaps they brought to this hour more than they found. But it is not enough to say that the experience was impressive to those of us who stood listening nearby. The music and the words permeated all the sensitive places in our souls. We all live with the awareness that there are emotional depths within us that cannot be expressed. In the scriptures that span the ages, the prophets have dwelt with delight on the scene yet to come: the day of reunion, when we are encircled in the arms of Christ's love. At that great finale, our hearts will be given the wings of song as one voice.

This is what prophets and patriarchs have called the "new song," the song of newness, "the song of redeeming love" (D&C 84:98; Alma 5:26). In that burst of harmony, we will rejoice in the echo of Christ's high-priestly prayer: "That they all may be one; as thou, Father, art in me, and I in thee, that they also may be one in us: that the world may believe that thou hast sent me" (John 17:21).

The at-one-ment of Jesus Christ achieves that all-inclusive oneness. There is no higher manifestation of love.

Fasting

JOHN AND JESUS ON FASTING

The portrait we have of John the Immerser is of a recluse—a hermit whose message and mien bring sounds of doom. It is repentance in sackcloth and ashes. It is mourning while wanting to be on the right side of imminent divine judgment. On the other hand, throughout his ministry, Jesus keeps saying that when the Bridegroom is with us, we eat and drink and even fast in the spirit of rejoicing.

Careful study will show that Jesus did not embrace nor endorse the piety-fasting of late Judaism or early Christianity. He and his recommended way of life were sometimes censured and condemned for this.[1] He still commends the good things of the earth "to please the eye and to gladden the heart . . . , to strengthen the body and to enliven the soul" (D&C 59:18–19). This does not extend to extortion (the last fig on the tree) nor to excessive indulgence to the point of gluttony. But for Jesus it is not unnatural or artificial to associate fasting with feasting—feasting on the Spirit of the Lord.

The preparation for such spiritual riches may require prayerful abstention. Then Spirit quickens us both in body and spirit. Jesus himself fasted before he ascended the Mount of Transfiguration and descended to conquer evil spirits. Fasting from food and feasting on the sacrament is the forecast of a glorious meal.

John was the harbinger of repentance in sackcloth and penitence. Jesus was pouring new wine in new wineskins to welcome the glad tidings of the new kingdom.

There is a time and place for "negative spirituality," for self-denial and austerity. Even for bleak postponements. But that is only part of his story. In the apocryphal Gospel of Thomas we are "to hold ourselves back from evil or pollution" (Logion 27). For several Book of Mormon prophets, and Christ himself, we are "to deny ourselves of all ungodliness" (Moroni 10:32; compare JST, Matthew 5:34). But godliness transcends chronic dejection or mortification.

---

1. See John Muddiman in Freedman, *Anchor Bible Dictionary,* 2:776.

OF FAST DAYS

Two days after Christmas, December 27, 1832, the saints were taught about fasting: "Also, I give unto you a commandment that ye shall continue in prayer and fasting from this time forth" (D&C 88:76). Later, the temple was described as "a house of fasting," as well as a house of prayer.

Detailing events of the winter of 1836–1837, Eliza R. Snow cites a Sabbath revelation that commends fasting "on my holy day." It also commends bringing to Sabbath meetings a glad heart and a cheerful countenance, "that thy fasting may be perfect" (D&C 59:13).

In her diary, Eliza wrote:

> Every first day of the week, the Temple was occupied by crowded assemblies. And on the first Thursday of each month, that day being observed strictly by the Latter-day Saints as the day of fasting and prayer.
>
> These meetings were hallowed and interesting beyond the power of language to describe. Many, many were the pentecostal seasons of the outpouring of the Spirit of God on those days, manifesting the gifts of the gospel, and the power of healing, prophesying, speaking in tongues, the interpretation of tongues, etc.
>
> I have there seen the lame man, on being administered to, throw aside his crutches and walk home perfectly healed; and not only were the lame made to walk, but the blind to see, the deaf to hear, the dumb to speak, and evil spirits to depart.[1]

---

1. *Biography and Family Record of Lorenzo Snow,* 12–13. See also Grant, *Kingdom of God Restored,* 199.

FASTING AND TRUST

Susa Young Gates, mother of thirteen children and author of 1,300 articles, wrote:

> I was one day talking with Bishop [Orson F.] Whitney, and he asked me if I had experienced the great power to be obtained through fasting and prayer. No, I had not. I had fasted on fast days, and sometimes I had fasted on the Sabbath, just for the general good I obtained. I had never tried fasting for special purposes to any extent, and I knew very little about it. He advised me to try fasting and see what marvelous results would flow from it. I began to do so.

> But in the midst of my experiences I found that quite frequently I fasted to obtain a certain blessing, which was not given directly, not at all sometimes, and yet I could always date back some important blessing as having been given to me, after a season of fasting and prayer. Gradually there began to dawn on my mind another principle, which I had always known through reading and hearing of it, but never had it come directly to my own heart.

> It was the very point spoken of by Brother John: that I must not seek to bend the will of God to suit my own desires.

> Lately there has come to me a most beautiful feeling of infinite trust and reliance upon every event that transpires in my life. It is all right; everything is all right. Sickness, thank God for that; health, thank God for that; poverty, thank God for that; wealth and pleasure, thank God for that. If a pleasure comes, thank God for it. If death raps at my door, thank God for that. If only I, this cumbersome, heavy, willful, disobedient I, can keep the laws of God, what is anything that happens to me? Nothing but a providence of God, and therefore to be received joyfully. The only sorrow I have is in contemplating my own backslidings.[1]

---

1. Gates, "Editor's Department," 570.

FASTING AND AID TO THE NEEDFUL

Joseph Smith taught that a true and faithful Christian "is to feed the hungry, to clothe the naked, to provide for the widow, to dry up the tear of the orphan, to comfort the afflicted, whether in this church, or in any other, or in no church at all, wherever he finds them."[1]

The principle of fasting and making an offering to assist the poor was established in the 1840s and has continued in the Church since then. For many years, most members of the Church were poor yet gave of their meager possessions to those less fortunate.

Giving the value of two meals not eaten during a fast was appropriate for the saints in their time of poverty. Presidents since have urged members to be very generous in giving to the poor. This may mean many times the value of two meals missed, depending on the financial abilities of the donor.

Blessings to all accrue from generosity to the poor.

"Let this be an ensample to all saints, and there will never be any lack of bread: When the poor are starving, let those who have, fast one day and give what they otherwise would have eaten to the bishops for the poor, and every one will abound for a long time; . . . And so long as the saints will all live this principle, with glad hearts and cheerful countenances they will always have an abundance."[2]

---

1. *Times and Seasons*, March 15, 1842.
2. Smith, *History of the Church*, 7:413.

OF UNION AND SURROUNDMENT

We meet together oft to take the sacrament. Why not alone?

Among the Hopis, when a person becomes ill, not just physically, but in his spirit—we would say when he is emotionally disturbed, down, or depressed—the tribe unites to fast for three days. They withdraw themselves from food and drink and purify themselves in "sweat huts." Then they consecrate a quantity of cornmeal, one part from each family, and it is mixed in a special way with buffalo meat. They then gather in a circle around the afflicted one and proceed to sing and dance and pray for long hours until the person, at the center of the circle, is visibly improved.

Thus concerted attention is given. The song of the whole tribe cares for him and with him. They are willing to share of their own "life force" (what they eat or don't eat) and of their own spirit in his aid. Their legends say that always the sufferer is made well.

All this echoes what the Lord has made clear. He puts a premium on united prayer. "Be agreed as touching all things whatsoever ye ask" (D&C 27:18). We are asked to cement in our minds the very words of those acting prayerfully in our behalf.

Is not this a refinement and embellishment of "uniting in fasting and prayer" and "uniting in the sacrament"?

Spiritually we are sometimes in need of immediate and intensive care.

Then we undertake to "bear ye one another's burdens, and so fulfil the law of Christ" (Galatians 6:2).

When we pray, many pray with us. So do some beyond the veil who know "our thoughts, motions, and feelings and are pained therewith."[1] In ways beyond our present ken they are able to combine efforts in our behalf. And we are taught by the modern Prophet that "by union of feeling we obtain power with God."[2]

---

1. *Words of Joseph Smith,* 254.
2. Ibid., 123.

Emblems

YE HAVE SEEN ME

Symbolism

Jesus was born in Bethlehem in surroundings that became for him, as for us, reminders of the measures of his mission.

He was born at night under a brilliant star. He would become the Light of the World.

He was born near grinding flour mills in a little town known as the house of bread. He would become the Living Bread, sent from heaven to revive the famished.

He was born at the edge of terraced pastures for sheep and lamb. He would become the Good Shepherd, the one who would never recoil from the disabilities and diseases of his flock.

He was born near Solomon's pools and the clay channels that supplied water to Jerusalem, the Holy City. He would offer the gift of Living Water, flowing to our inner deserts when bereft of love and care.

He was born amidst ancient olive trees and oil presses. He would become *Ha Maschiac*—the Anointed One—who would pour soothing oil into the wounds of body and spirit.[1]

He was born only a few steps from the age-old footpath of Abraham, who trudged with his son Isaac toward the mountain of the Lord. He would be called "the Lamb slain from the foundation of the world" (Revelation 13:8). And as he turned death into immortality, he would say, "I am the life" (John 11:25).

These are the beginning fulfillments of the words: "Behold, . . . all things are created and made to bear record of me" (Moses 6:63). Those who have eyes to see, see him everywhere.

---

1. See Luke 4:14–21; 3 Nephi 9:15.

HEAVENLY MANNA

When the children of the Exodus first saw manna—they had neither the foresight nor the time to prepare provisions for the wilderness—they said, "What is it?" (Exodus 16:15, note a).

Moses had to tell them, "This is the bread which the Lord hath
given you to eat" (Exodus 16:15).

It looked like coriander seed and had to be ground and boiled and
baked. Even then it was hardly palatable.

"Now the rabble that was among them had a strong craving; and
the people of Israel also wept again, and said, O that we had meat to
eat! We remember the fish we ate in Egypt for nothing, the cucumbers,
the melons, the leeks, the onions, and the garlic; but now our strength
is dried up, and there is nothing at all but this manna to look at." But it
was enough.

Jesus would later say, "Your fathers did eat manna in the wilderness,
and are dead. This is the bread which cometh down from heaven, that a
man may eat thereof, and not die" (John 6:49–50).

The priestly blessings on the tokens of bread and water change what
we prepare to what he prepares. For he promises that with our alert
partaking, his Spirit will enter us. It is "sanctified"—blessed and sanctified—to our souls. Not just to our bodies. Nor just to our minds and
spirits. It is dedicated to the soul, which is the whole of us.

Sufficient unto the day—but not more than a day—was the manna
thereof. And sufficient unto the week is the sacrament thereof. As
Hyrum Smith taught:

"When the sacrament will be administered in the Lord's house, it
will do away with a great deal of difficulty that is now in existence . . .
when you offer up your sacraments every Sabbath, you will feel well a
whole week; you will get a great portion of the Spirit of God, enough
to last you a week, and you will increase enough to last a whole week."[1]

---

1. In *Times and Seasons,* August 1, 1844.

LEAVEN AND UNLEAVENED BREAD

Over the millennia, biblical writers have interpreted yeast or *pesakhim* as like a powerful seed. It is somehow alive and pervasive as it spreads. Yeast turns hard, unpalatable grain-become-dough into bread. A yeastlike element turns grapes into delicious wine. It is the veritable symbol of life itself.

During the week of the Passover—today as anciently—the custom is to remove and abandon all traces of yeast in kitchen, home, and table. Even the crumbs of soft, fulsome, chewy breads and rolls are ferreted out and discarded.

What remains is the dry, flat matza. It looks and tastes like thick cardboard. It reminds of the hardships of the delivered children of Israel, who fled Egypt in haste—no time for the bread to rise. Behind them were the verdant fields of the overflowing Nile. Before them was the severe desert.

As the Passover feast is a feast of unleavened bread, so the sacrament is a feast of leavened bread. Christ's life and spirit are the leavening. We are reminded that his good earth—not without labor—produces nutriment that is tasty and fulfilling. His life gives zest and tingle and vibrancy to the saints in the midst of their modern wilderness. The Savior is the savor of all that enters us. Without his pervasive leaven, without his life powers, we slowly wither.

Often we do not realize how hungry and thirsty we are until we eat and drink.

THE WINEPRESS

There are several ways to tread out the grapes in a wine vat:

You can shackle a beast of burden, a burro or donkey. On its feet put burlap "shoes." Then prod it in circular or back-and-forth stomping motions. Or you can bring a large angled stone and, with hand and foot, tip it back and forth with twisting or grinding motions. Or you can join arms with strong men for ballast and hold on to straps from a supporting beam, and tramp, tramp, tramp together.

Finally, lacking all these, you can step in barefoot and tread alone. But the vat is dangerously slippery. Very quickly, tender feet blister and tear from the seeds and stems.

How did Jesus do it? He did it as Isaiah foresaw. He did it in the hardest of hard ways: "I have trodden the winepress alone" (Isaiah 63:3).

We will comprehend this when he comes again: "The Lord shall be red in his apparel, and his garments like him that treadeth in the wine-vat. . . . And his voice shall be heard: I have trodden the wine-press alone, and have brought judgment upon all people; and none were with me" (D&C 133:48, 50).

On that day, "so great shall be the glory of his presence that the sun shall hide his face in shame, and the moon shall withhold its light, and the stars shall be hurled from their places" (D&C 133:49).

When we drink faithfully of the pure wine of the vine, we anticipate the glory of his presence. We are promised—now and not just hereafter—"the life and the light, the Spirit and the power, sent forth by the will of the Father through Jesus Christ, his Son" (D&C 50:27).

At last we may be fully with him.

THE OIL OF GLADNESS

We have watched men and women in the valley of the Kidron shake olives loose or "beat" them off the tree with long sticks or clubs. The olives fall onto cloths or robes spread underneath. If you pick up a green olive in its prime, and dare to bite into it, the taste is bitter, almost like a burn. The tongue recoils in pain. At least two thousand years before Jesus, the people had learned to gather olives and place them in the *yam,* the olive crusher, and rotate a millstone up to fifty times until they had an oily mash. (There is some oil even in the pits.)

I once stood with a biochemist before a reconstructed olive press. "Explain to me the chemical process that turns harsh, acrid olives into sweet oil," I asked.

"It is not a chemical process," he said. "It is pressure."

He knew the way. The mash is put in circular hemp baskets and placed under a winch with a huge pendulum. Four or more men strain together to twist the winch all the way down. Oil begins to ooze into a small cauldron or tub. Shortly the water, and with it the acidic bitterness, separates from the oil, and the oil rises to the top.

Moses was instructed, "And thou shalt command the children of Israel, that they bring thee pure oil olive beaten for the light, to cause the lamp to burn always" (Exodus 27:20). So we understand that Jesus himself was beaten for the light, bringing the oil to us. Olive oil creates light amidst darkness.

Olive oil had two other sacred uses: first, for anointing kings and prophets—more penetrating and qualifying than a jeweled crown. It was the Lord's stamp or token or seal of official callings (see Leviticus 8:6–12). Second, like a prepared poultice, it was used in the hour of sickness for wounds and bruises for healing.

Jesus who knelt in Gethsemane—the place of the olive press (*gat* = garden; *shemen* = oil)—provides all three of these divine boons. He is the Anointed One and, through his Spirit and ordinances, he is the Anointing One.

LIVING WATER AND PURITY

Few think of the Holy Land as a land of many waters. But at the base of Mount Hermon in the area of the Banyas, water not only seeps or flows but gushes through several waterfalls. It then flows to the violin-shaped Kenneret, the Sea of Galilee, on which the very life of the land and its people depends.

Streams of water are to make glad the city of God, the dwelling-place of the Most High. Jerusalem is to be an Edenic garden. Its own flowing waters will fructify but also purify. Someday, Zechariah predicts, "a fountain [shall be] opened to the house of David and to the inhabitants of Jerusalem for sin and for uncleanness" (Zechariah 13:1).

According to a long-standing tradition, living water is freshly drawn water. It is the water of the running stream, in contrast to the water of the stagnant cistern or pool. Stream water is associated with cleansing rituals.

In the time of Jesus (and continuing to our day), at the end of harvest and at the beginning of the new water year, the Feast of Tabernacles was celebrated. A water-drawing ceremony was performed.

It was at that time, standing near the temple amidst blazing torches of light, that Jesus announced that he himself is a source of the promised living water.

During other festivals Jesus had promised abundance—bread during the days of Passover, and light as he gave sight to the blind man.

His timing, his intent, and his offering were all evocative of living water. "One of the soldiers with a spear pierced his side, and forthwith came there out blood and water" (John 19:34).

In these and all other ways he is the manifestation of life.

"OF YOUR OWN MAKE"

In the sacrament, we consume tokens of the Savior's real flesh and blood. The Spirit then honors our remembrance. With it comes a cluster of feelings and resolves and appeals to our best selves.

The emblems of the sacrament are products of the good earth, "that which cometh of the earth" (D&C 49:19), and of hard labor—much labor.

To forge wheat into bread, we must plant, nurture, harvest, separate wheat kernels from the chaff, grind them into flour, introduce the leaven, and then fire and bake.

Likewise, wine emerges from painstaking vine-planting, nurturing, grafting, pruning, harvesting, and treading out the grapes.

If we do none of these but purchase the emblems, that too represents earnings from labor that takes a toll on the resources and energies of both men and women.

In modern revelation Jesus commends the use of "pure wine of the grape of the vine, of your own make" (D&C 89:6). The narration of his visitation among the Nephites tells us it was of his own make. For when he provided the sacrament, the people brought nothing, neither bread nor wine. He provided it all. We are not told how (see 3 Nephi 20:6–7).

So we are to understand that with us, Jesus himself is a bread-maker. And Jesus is a wine-maker.

In the sweat of our face we prepare the bread and wine. In the sweat of his face—a bloody sweat—he sanctifies them to our souls.

"BEHOLD, I MAKE ALL THINGS NEW"

Who of us does not yearn for the power of a fresh start, a clean slate, a new lease on life? The vital elements of sacramental observance, and the higher ordinances of the temple, are comprehended in one word: *new*.

The restored gospel is itself good news. And *news* is the plural of *new*.

Authentic saints are newborn. And "being born again comes by the Spirit of God through ordinances."[1] They are enlivened by walking a lively and better way.

The new wine of revelation is being poured into new bottles. Old and misleading traditions fall away.

Christ, "the mediator of the new covenant" (D&C 76:69), is giving "a new commandment" (D&C 56:5) and "a new commission" (D&C 75:7). Temples manifest his new and everlasting covenant.

There will be a New Jerusalem, and a restoring of the old Jerusalem.

Eventually the faithful will inherit "a new heaven and a new earth" (D&C 29:23; see also 63:49).

In sum, we are approaching a day when "old things shall pass away, and all things shall become new" (D&C 29:24). So it is altogether fitting that sacramental emblems be bread newly made or, in any case, newly broken, and wine to be "pure wine of the grape of the vine," and "made new among you" (D&C 89:6; 27:4).

---

1. *Words of Joseph Smith,* 12.

THE COMMON CUP

In the early days of the Church, the sacrament was sometimes administered from a common cup, passed for a sip, row by row, to each member.

Twelve such cups were carefully made for sacrament services held each Sabbath in the Salt Lake Tabernacle. The people surrendered silver items, jewelry, watches, and spoons, which were turned by silversmiths into the large cups. Each had double handles. Matching plates, later baskets, were used for the bread.

"Are ye able to drink of the cup that I shall drink of?" Jesus asked his disciples.

He answered his own question—in one sense you cannot. But in one sense you can.

"And he saith unto them, Ye shall drink indeed of my cup, and be baptized with the baptism that I am baptized with: but to sit on my right hand, and on my left, is not mine to give, but it shall be given to them for whom it is prepared of my Father" (Matthew 20:22–23).

In Semitic languages, *cup* has the same root as the word for door or vestibule or entryway. "The cup" in antiquity was the figure of one's role in life, one's condition or one's destiny—favorable or not. It remains the metaphor of a divinely appointed role, whether of prosperity or adversity.

Today we lift individualized cups to our lips. They are a token of his own cup, a token of what entered and afflicted his soul. As if the words were inscribed, "In all their afflictions he was afflicted . . . and in his love, and in his pity, he redeemed them, and bore them, and carried them all the days of old" (D&C 133:53).

By design, our partaking hastens our release and relief and fulfillment.

Of his long days and nights he says to us now, "Glory be to the Father, and I partook and finished my preparations unto the children of men" (D&C 19:19).

He has made all the necessary preparations for all of us.

LAMB

In Nephi's interchange with the angel, a vision of the future redemptive life of Jesus was given. Not fewer than fifty times the angel uses the name/title "Lamb" for Christ (see 1 Nephi 11–14).

A lamb is frisky, impulsive, easily misled. It is vulnerable to the ravages of climate, the predatory wolf, and the jackal. Other hazards are the waterless desert, separation, and dangers that lurk at night outside the fold.

Why, of all things, would Jesus be named a lamb? Because he is the classic example of weak things becoming strong in the hand of God. From infancy as a lambkin to the triumphal Lamb, he "[overcame] the world" (John 16:33). He was the Lamb preappointed to be slain "from before the foundation of the world" (Moses 5:57). And then to triumph.

"And I looked, and, lo, a Lamb stood on the mount Sion" (Revelation 14:1).

At the peak of our communion in temple dedications, we cry out a prayer of redemption. We cry to the one invincible source for our overcoming mortality and inheriting Jesus's high privileges. We do not shout hosanna to God alone, but hosanna "to God and the Lamb" (D&C 76:119; see also verses 21, 39, 85). His lamb. Our lamb.

When is he most powerful in enabling us to overcome? When we become lamblike. This is a quiet and private miracle. It is the encounter of those who truly know themselves and know their Shepherd. It is possible because the Lamb is the leading Shepherd. All lambs who follow him, as they are guided by him, become shepherds and shepherdesses.

Otherwise we tend to wander and wonder in vain, and we miss the brighter tones of life. And of love. And of light.

Those who have deliberately and needfully entered his fold can acknowledge that "all we like sheep have gone astray" (Isaiah 53:6). Yet to the degree that we emulate him, it can be said, "All we like shepherds have found the way."

THE VINE

In the region of Caesarea Philippi, near a rushing stream of blue-white water, is an enormous vine. It has the diameter of a small tree. For decades it has wound itself around nearby trees in every direction for hundreds of feet. But there is not a blossom, nor a grape. It has all gone to wood. First prize for size, but fruitless.

Jesus teaches that such a vine must be pruned, even severely pruned, to become fruitful. Otherwise it will be "hewn down, and cast into the fire."[1] For barren vines only encumber the vineyard.

In his last parable to his closest disciples, Jesus says, "I am the vine, ye are the branches." And "Ye cannot bear fruit except ye abide in me." And "Without me ye can do nothing." If they break off from the true and living Vine they will wither (John 15).

Here Jesus combines images: "abide, abode, abound, and abundance." He promises the Holy Ghost, "even upon you my friends that it may *abide in your hearts* even the Holy Spirit of promise" (D&C 88:3). He promises that "if a man love me, he will keep my words: and my father will love him, and we [both me and my father] will . . . m*ake our abode* with him" (John 14:23). He promises that we can come to "know that I am, and that I am the true light that is in you, otherwise *you could not abound"* (D&C 88:50). He announces, "I am come that [ye] might have life, and *that [ye] might have it more abundantly"* (John 10:10).

John summarizes, "He that hath the Son hath life; and he that hath not the Son of God hath not life" (1 John 5:12).

"And now, little children, abide in him" (1 John 2:28).

It is not enough to stay close to the trunk. To be fruit-bearing, we must stay connected, permanently, to the fruitful Vine.[2]

---

1. Jesus in Matthew 7:19; Luke 3:9. Compare D&C 45:50, 57; 97:7.
2. See *Words of Joseph Smith,* 13–15.

OF PISTACHIO OIL

Gifts are the essence of the nativity celebration.

Gold, frankincense, and myrrh (all three present in the holy of holies in the temple) were bestowed by the magi at Christ's birth (see Matthew 2:11). What of the gift just before his death?

It was from an alabaster container. And costly. The worth of a year's wages. That brought grumbling to the lips of others who considered this lavish and extravagant. Mary might have used a little. But in a gesture that had ritual precedent she bestowed it all on his head and feet (see John 12:3–8).

He himself said it: "She did it for my burial" (Matthew 26:12).

The ointment most likely was not purchased. It was more probably blended by her own mastery of oils and scented leaves, a mixture of balsam and pistachio and perhaps also the balm of Gilead from trees beyond the Jordan.

Was this Mary of Bethany also Mary of Magdala? Was her relationship with him, as an apocryphal account says, so close that Jesus asked her to accompany him to the tomb where she witnessed the raising of Lazarus?

This was the miracle that would set the neighborhood in an uproar and so stun officialdom that they vowed Jesus must be stopped or the whole world would begin to believe.

Pistis in Greek means faith. Mary's bestowal of pistachio oil was the token of her tender trust in Jesus and his mission.

She gave her gift to the man who had and has everything—everything to give. Life eternal.

OFFERING SALT

On Shabbat Eve, the rabbi or father blesses and breaks the bread. He then salts it and gives it by hand to his wife and to his children. The practice goes back to a prescription in Leviticus, "With all thine offerings thou shalt offer salt" (Leviticus 2:13).

Jesus identifies salt with savor and teaches that without its savor salt is good for nothing, only to be trodden under foot. He identifies salt with life and says, "I will liken [life] unto salt which is good" (JST, Luke 14:36). He identifies the savor of salt with "Savior" and promises that there is a way we can, in a measure, join him in his role (see D&C 101:39).

All this is not mere wordplay. He assures us we can be the salt of the earth, a blessing to the human family starting with our own. We can understand further:

- Salt is spiritually and externally a preservative of goodness and beauty.
- It not only enhances taste from bland to delicious, but makes most foods and sauces better. ("Salt is what makes things taste bad when it isn't in them.")
- Salt is curative: it smarts and stings on open wounds, yet in due time it soothes and heals.
- As a poet noticed, in a close-up photo of a tear—a tear is salt water—one sees a pattern like a cross.

Tears of disappointment and grief burn the cheeks, but tears of relief kiss them. Tears of gladness and surprise show that we have been touched. And sometimes we shed tears of unutterable thanks.

For the saints, weeping is permitted, even commanded. "Thou shalt weep for the loss of them that die" (D&C 42:45). Jesus wept both in sorrow and in joy. So, on occasion, did the surrounding multitudes. The sacramental life can help us fulfill the counsel attributed to Boris Pasternak: "Be so close that when others weep you taste salt." Especially when the most significant other is Christ.

THE LEES "WELL REFINED"

A huge wine-making complex has been discovered in the Holy Land. It is in the area of Ashkelon near the sea. One hundred presses, buried for centuries, testify to an industry that flourished 350 years before Christ. Wine jugs of four- to five-gallon capacity were fired in the kilns of the area. Millions of them were produced and exported. One winepress or vat was huge: 2,650 square feet. Many men over long periods would have had to labor in this vat, chiseled out of the limestone.

The best wine was made from juice that trickled out without pressing or squeezing. The next wine required treading heavily, sometimes with bare feet, until the liquid could be scooped out of the vat. The last, bitter and barely palatable wine came from the pulp made up of grape stems and the seeds. They were placed under immense pressure in a twisting-down or rotating press. The result was "the dregs," sometimes called "the lees," the final sediment or residue of the winepress.

He who said, "I have trodden the winepress alone" (Isaiah 63:3); he who said, "Would that I might not drink the bitter cup, and shrink" (D&C 19:18); he who said, "I have drunk out of that bitter cup which the Father hath given me" (3 Nephi 11:11); he who drank it to the very dregs now invites us to a feast "on the lees" in the land of Zion.

"And also that a feast of fat things might be prepared for the poor; yea, a feast of fat things, of wine on the lees well refined, that the earth may know that the mouths of the prophets shall not fail; Yea, a supper of the house of the Lord, well prepared, unto which all nations shall be invited" (D&C 58:8).

He drank the bitter that we might drink the sweet.

OIL LAMPS AND FLAMES

In the midst of a revelation on the promised Second Coming of Christ we are counseled:

"Wherefore, be faithful, praying always,

"having your lamps trimmed" (the burnt or sooty part of the wick cut away so it will burn clean and almost smokeless)

"and burning," (alight and afire)

"and oil with you," (a reserve juglet of extra oil to last through the night; a typical filled lamp can last at most five hours; the foolish virgins did not have this crucial reserve oil)

all this, "that you may be ready at the coming of the Bridegroom" (D&C 33:17).

An oil lamp is curved like the bottom half of an avocado, small enough to fit in the palm of the hand, large enough to burn steadily through many hours—but not all night.

It is alight enough to penetrate a stretch of darkness ahead, and to prevent stumbling or bumping or slipping.

It is bright enough to reach every corner in the most expansive room.

It is steady enough, if the wick is trimmed, to continue with a gem-like flame even against the grain of a brisk wind.

One crucial verse is added by Joseph Smith to the double prophecy of Matthew 24: "And whoso treasureth up my word, shall not be deceived" (Joseph Smith—Matthew 1:37). The Psalmist writes, "Thy word is a lamp unto my feet, and a light unto my path" (Psalm 119:105).

The oil lamp is a lasting invitation to take the Holy Spirit as our guide.

"For they that are wise and have received the truth, and have taken the Holy Spirit for their guide, and have not been deceived—verily I say unto you, they shall not be hewn down and cast into the fire, but shall abide the day" (D&C 45:57).

Glorious Modern Precedents

TUESDAY SACRAMENT: FIRST IN THE CHURCH

It was a Tuesday, the third day of the week, the day described in the creation narratives when God pronounced twice the words, "It is good." (Even now it is the preferred day for Jewish couples to be married.) It is the day in New Testament lore that Jesus attended a wedding feast and performed his first miracle: water to wine. It became the appointed day when the Bridegroom began making preparations for his return.

On that day, Tuesday, the sixth of April, 1830, the Church was organized. The history says, "We then took bread, blessed it and brake it with them: also wine, blessed it, and drank it with them. We then laid our hands on each individual member of the Church present, that they might receive the gift of the Holy Ghost, and be confirmed members of the Church of Christ."

The sacrament prayers were those recorded by Moroni as "gems for the sanctified" before he sealed up the record. That day a revelation confirmed that these prayers were to be used henceforth in the Church (see D&C 20:77, 79).

"The Holy Ghost was poured out upon us to a very great degree—some prophesied whilst we all praised the Lord, and rejoiced exceedingly."

Elsewhere the record says, "The Spirit of God rested upon the congregation, and great solemnity prevailed."[1]

---

1. Smith, *History of the Church*, 2:433.

CARRYING THE FIRE AT KIRTLAND

Describing the outpourings at meetings at the Kirtland Temple in 1835, Erastus Snow, later one of the Twelve, records that "all the Lord's anointed" assembled therein and received the ordinance of the washing of feet. (In order, the Prophet said, that "we may be one in feeling and sentiment."[1])

They met from morning until evening and from evening until morning. Some beheld angels. Some spoke in and interpreted the gift of tongues, and "cloven tongues like fire sat upon many of them." Some prophesied as the Spirit gave utterance.

> In the evening they would eat the passover, and feasted upon bread and wine until they were filled, and after these things were over, the disciples went from house to house, breaking bread and eating it with joyful hearts, being full of the spirit of prophecy, and the sick were healed and devils were cast out.[2]

Similarly, at the Kirtland School of the Prophets. Zebedee Coltrin recalls:

> The salutation as written in the D&C [88:136–141] was carried out at that time, and at every meeting, and the washing of feet was attended to, the sacrament was also administered at times when Joseph appointed, after the ancient order.
>
> Every time we were called together to attend to any business, we came together in the morning about sunrise, fasting and partook of the sacrament each time, and before going to school we washed ourselves and put on clean linen.[3]

---

1. *Teachings of the Prophet Joseph Smith*, 91.
2. Erastus Snow, *Sketchbook*, 8.
3. Minutes, SLC School of Prophets, October 3, 1883, 56.

A FEAST AT KIRTLAND

In Kirtland days, Joseph Smith planned a feast for the poor with Newel K. Whitney, a presiding shepherd or pastor (bishop) of the Church. Whitney had overcome, as the Prophet predicted he would, his tendencies to be "narrow of heart and covetous."

Together they acted in the pattern of the "ancient order," referring to early Israelite practice. Because of his own poverty, Joseph did not have a home of his own and was himself a guest, albeit an honored guest. These brethren joined arms, fetched and carried, set tables, cooked and washed and participated in inviting, welcoming, and seating the guests.

Few in that small and bereft community were affluent or well-off. The poor and crippled, the halt and the blind and the maimed (see Luke 14:21), were invited. The meal was modest. For the guests anything more than hominy and milk was a novelty and a delicacy. The partaking was accompanied by prayer and song. Joseph, like the ancient Abraham, "stood by" (meaning never sat down) as the servant of all.

Says the record, "Our hearts were made glad while partaking of an antepast of those joys that will be poured out upon the heads of the Saints when they are gathered together on Mount Zion, to enjoy each other's society forevermore, when there will be none to molest or make us afraid."[1]

Joseph said often to Mother Whitney that no meal in his life had been more richly fulfilling than this summons of the needy and the underprivileged to a bounteous table-altar in her humble home. The meal was a way of showing love as in ancient agape feasts.[2]

---

1. *Personal Writings of Joseph Smith*, 62.
2. See "Love Feasts," in Freedman, *Anchor Bible Dictionary.*

GUIDELINES AT FAR WEST

Wine was used in the sacrament in Kirtland and in Missouri, and continued to be used until the day Joseph the Prophet was instructed "to buy no more wine of the enemies for the sacrament, but use water, until they should make wine new themselves for their enemies would try to kill the saints with poison in wine."[1]

Oliver Huntington recorded this recollection of Philo Dibble. It was of a Sabbath in Far West, Missouri, June or July, 1838. He writes:

> The Prophet Joseph Smith gave the people a true pattern—A pattern of the true manner of partaking of the sacrament. The people came together in the morning without their breakfast, to the bowery on the Public Square where there was prepared a plenty of good bread and a barrel of wine. The bread and wine was blessed. Every person ate bread and drank wine as they wanted all day, when they wanted. They sat and talked, and walked and conversed upon heavenly and spiritual things as they felt like.
>
> [They] walked out on the Prairie and returned to eat and drink. No one said "Let's go and get a drink" but with solemnity they commemorated the death and sufferings of Jesus.
>
> A part of the day Joseph was preaching in the large room on the North side of the square, while George A. Smith preached on the South side, from a wagon. No one was intoxicated during the day.[2]

---

1. Oliver B. Huntington diary, 37; Church History Library.
2. Philo Dibble diary; Church History Library.

AMIDST THE EXILES IN COMMERCE, ILLINOIS

The journal of Joseph Smith for 1839 records his day-by-day struggles after his escape from the squalor of Liberty Jail. This period involved the movement of the saints to Quincy, Illinois. Then began city-building in the river bottoms of Nauvoo. The people had been hounded, uprooted, shaken.

In late autumn of 1839, Joseph's entries report malaria and "ague." He writes, for example, "About this time sickness began to manifest itself much amongst the brethren as well as among the inhabitants of the place, so that this week and the following was generally spent in visiting the sick, and administering unto them. Some had faith enough and were healed, others had not." Priesthood administrations continued in the weeks afterward and included visits to the bedridden in nearby Montrose.

On a later Sunday, Joseph records, "I spoke and admonished the church individually to set his house in order, to make clean the inside of the platter, and to meet on the next Sabbath to partake of the sacrament in order that by our obedience to the ordinances, we might be enabled to prevail with God against the destroyer, and that the sick may be healed."

This was a turning point. From then on, administering to the sick became more effectual. "The people," Joseph wrote, "are gaining strength and recovering health." A week later Joseph recorded "sickness decreasing." In the following week, "This week sickness much decreased." And finally on a Sunday he records, "All in general recovering but some very slowly."[1]

---

1. See pages 7, 8, and 9 of Joseph Smith's minute book for 1839; L. Tom Perry Special Collections, Brigham Young University.

AT ZARAHEMLA, IOWA

As the community of gathering saints expanded the limits of Nauvoo, some moved into Iowa. Joseph encouraged these scattered settlements to consolidate just across the river from Nauvoo. In March 1841 came the word, "Let them build up a city unto my name upon the land opposite the city of Nauvoo, and let the name of Zarahemla be named upon it . . . that they may be prepared for that which is in store for a time to come" (D&C 125:2–3).

To the instruction, Joseph added an ominous note: "You have Haun's Mill for a sample." They began to understand the risks, spiritual and temporal, of being a vulnerable distant outpost. Scattering had other consequences.

William Clayton wrote that "the saints frequently told us that the devil was over the river but this did not hinder us from going." They found the people, as had been rumored, were "having no meetings, full of envy, strife and contention and in a very bad state."

Uncle John Smith visited nearby Montrose. "He called upon all who had hardness and who had transgressed to confess and repent. He stated that about twelve months ago he had appointed them a person to take charge of the meeting and administer the sacrament which he had only attended to once since that time. After many had confessed he called upon myself (Clayton) and brother Nickerson to break bread and administer which was done. And we hope it will be continued faithfully hereafter."[1]

---

1. *William Clayton's Journal,* 14–16.

ELIZA ON THE PLAINS

On April 7, 1846, somewhere west of Nauvoo, Eliza R. Snow participated in the first sacrament meeting of the exiles since they left the temple behind. She describes it as a sacrament "of him whom I desire to behold. O, Jesus, let me soon behold thy face."[1]

The next day Heber C. Kimball came to her "study" in her prairie schooner. In the spirit of prayer and blessing he assured her, "A father's blessing shall rest upon you from this time." (Her parents by now were gone, as was her husband, Joseph. And she was childless.)

She made her way as an ascent. She traveled under a sense of mission. As she left Winter Quarters on January 6, Eliza's journal registers no complaints: "I had a time not to be forgotten. My heart was filled to overflowing with gratitude to my father in heaven. I spoke and then interpreted. I then blessed the girls in a song, singing to each in rotation."

June 1, 1847, not far from the valley, she describes another Sabbath gathering: "Had a powerful time. Deep things were brought forth which were not to be spoken."

After another such meeting she wrote, "My feelings were very peculiar through the day. It verily seemed that the glory of God rested down on the wagons and overspread the prairie."

Cruel elements required daily stamina. Yet, who can say the faithful were to be pitied? They felt they were walking under divine counsel and aid. They knew spiritual elation in the midst of affliction.

---

1. Eliza R. Snow journal; Church History Library.

NEAR INDEPENDENCE ROCK

"When the vanguard company had traveled 514½ miles from Winter Quarters, they halted near a stream of clear water."

It was a Sabbath. Wilford Woodruff wrote in his journal:

> At nine o'clock most of the brethren retired a little south of the camp and had a prayer meeting, and as many as chose to, expressed their feelings. At a little before twelve they met again in the same spot to partake of the sacrament.
>
> Then the camp went onto the bluffs and selecting a small, circular, level spot surrounded by bluffs and out of sight, we clothed ourselves in the priestly garments and offered up prayer to God for ourselves, this camp and all pertaining to it, the brethren in the army [Mormon Battalion], our families and all the saints, President Young being mouth. We all felt well and glad for this privilege.
>
> When we started for the bluffs, there was a heavy black thunder cloud rising from the southwest, and from all appearance it might rain any minute, but the brethren believed it would not rain till we got through and if it did we chose rather to take a wetting than to be disappointed of the privilege. It kept off remarkably till we got through and got our regular clothing on, but soon after it began to rain and after we got to camp it rained considerably, accompanied by strong wind.
>
> I never noticed the brethren so still and sober on a Sunday since we started as today. There is no jesting nor laughing, nor nonsense. All appear to be sober and feel to remember their covenant which makes things look far more pleasant than they have done heretofore.[1]

---

1. Wilford Woodruff journal, Church Archives.

IN THE WAKE OF THE SALT LAKE
TEMPLE DEDICATION

In the upper rooms of the dedicated Salt Lake Temple, 115 priesthood leaders joined in a prayer circle. It was the first held in this temple of temples, and the largest ever held in this dispensation. Then the sacrament was administered, brother to brother. B. H. Roberts wrote in his journal: "Thus was the Lord's supper truly the sacrament. And we ate and drank in memory of Him—our Savior and Redeemer, our Advocate with the Father. Every face beamed with happiness and shone with intelligence."[1]

Of this gathering Abraham Cannon wrote: "It was a very happy and never to be forgotten time."[2] And Marriner W. Merrill: "We had a glorious time and all felt well."[3] And Erastus Snow: "All feeling full of the Spirit, in some instances too full for utterance. After supper we sang a hymn, conversed at pleasure and told our duties and told anecdotes principally of the Prophet Joseph. One could have sat I know not how long but as all things seem to have an end in this world so did this our meeting."[4]

As he reflected on this experience, B. H. Roberts wrote, "There seemed to flow into my soul a whole flood of light. This has been a Pentecostal time with me. The Lord has shown me my inner parts, myself; and there I have found such grained and gnarled spots that I have been humbled to sincere repentance. At times I have wondered even how the Lord could tolerate me at all as His servant. Truly it is a manifestation of longsuffering and mercy."[5]

In due time, solemn assemblies including sacramental worship were extended throughout the earth.

---

1. B. H. Roberts personal journal, April 1893; Church History Library.
2. A. H. Cannon journal, Thursday, 10 April 1893.
3. Marriner W. Merrill, 1937.
4. Erastus Snow diary, 165.
5. B. H. Roberts personal journal.

IN THE HOUR OF SORROWS

It was the beginning of a new year and a new century, 1900.

The brethren met in the Salt Lake Temple. The Church, its members and its leaders, had endured some of the worst shocks human flesh can take.

President Lorenzo Snow, age eighty-six and weighed down with responsibility, was coping with national outrage and vituperation, searing poverty, and the imprisonment of many Latter-day Saints. Some were saying the Church could not survive, let alone flourish.

The President spoke of "all kinds of troubles, both of heart burnings and of all kinds of sacrifices." Yet he added, "We have never lost hope of arriving at a state of perfect union." He reminded his brethren of a saying of Hyrum Smith, that when persecution ceases we forget the first commandment: to bring heart, mind, and strength to the love of God.

He then said he could look into the future with the greatest assurance. He did not feel to worry one particle as to the present or the future; in fact, it was almost impossible to imagine that the future could bring us greater troubles than we have already passed through. Everything considered, who, he asked, had so great reason for thanksgiving and rejoicing as we? All those present then partook of "the emblems of our Lord and Savior Jesus."[1]

So the sacrament has been administered amidst hardships and pain. And likewise amidst steady trust that relief and release will appear on the horizon.

Thus our table is spread "in the presence of our enemies," inside and out.

If we do not reach to him with whatever gladness we can muster, we may never know in this life what gladness is. He has provided the way.

---

1. Office journal of Lorenzo Snow, 1900, 8.

SACRAMENT IN ORBIT

Don Lind, astronaut, spoke of his awareness of what the Creator did for us as the Creator of our earth: "That was one of the most moving experiences of my life."

Another experience that is very close to me was to have the sacrament in orbit. We were in space for a full week, so of course, we were up there on a Sunday. Our bishop had given me permission to hold my own sacrament service. It was a little unusual. You priests in the audience might consider what it would be like to try to kneel down in weightlessness—you keep drifting off. For privacy I held my sacrament service in my sleep station—something like a Pullman berth. I kneeled on what you would think of as the ceiling and braced my shoulders against my sleeping bag so I would not float away. It was a very special experience. I will remember that sacrament service and the renewing of my baptismal covenants high above the earth all my life. It had some of that special feeling that you usually have only when you go to the temple.

Shortly after the flight I had the opportunity to show Sister Sharlene Wells, our Miss America, around the space center. She asked me if it didn't seem uncomfortable going into space upside down. I explained that in space you always feel right side up and stationary. The earth turns below you. If somebody's head is pointing toward your feet, he is the one who is upside down. At lift-off, the earth simply rotates to a position above your head, but that is the earth's problem.

Later at a fireside, Sister Wells made a comment about that situation that I think is very meaningful. In many things we do, the world thinks we are completely upside down. They think our moral values are foolish, our standards are restrictive, and our beliefs are quaint but outdated. The important thing is that we make sure that we keep ourselves right side up, aligned with the Lord, even if it makes the whole world look upside down.[1]

---

1. Lind, "The Heavens Declare," 39.

A SOLEMN ASSEMBLY

We gathered in the sanctuary, the "upper room" of the temple, local leaders more than 1,700 strong. For nearly an hour we sat in silence heavier than air—we could hear the silence—prepared to "worship the Lord in the beauty of holiness" (1 Chronicles 16:29).

Our brethren of the First Presidency and the Twelve entered, dressed in unadorned but immaculate white, and sat before us.

As they stood to break bread we sang the words of Eliza R. Snow: "How great the wisdom and the love that . . . sent the Savior from above."[1]

The apostles embraced the role of priests and deacons. As servants they were reenacting the counsels of Jesus—"that which ye have seen me do" (3 Nephi 18:24).

Most of us knew that the oldest of these brethren (David B. Haight) was struggling with blindness and that another (Neal A. Maxwell) was fighting with leukemia for his life. These two knelt to offer the sacrament prayers inherited from authentic ancient sources.

Then, row by row reaching out to us, they led us to consecrate ourselves anew in the private space of our own inner lives. As they brought the emblems their faces reflected the genuine care and kindness of their Master.

This, I imagined, was the feeling of fellowship, of *koinonia* (Greek) that attended table feasts in the infant Church in Jerusalem. Their whole lives were drawn together in common.

We were commissioned to "take home" what we felt and what we learned to our families and extended families.

In the latter days we have been charged, "Be one; and if ye are not one ye are not mine" (D&C 38:27). That often seems an unreachable imperative.

But that day, in this epitome of worship, we were one. And in the ways that matter most, ever since.

---

1. *Hymns*, no. 195.

Effects and Influences

I AM THE LIGHT; YE ARE THE LIGHT

A recent article on astronomy shows that there are within reach of our telescopes stars that are one trillion times brighter than our sun! None of us can stand one-trillionth of that light for more than a few hours.

Does this strengthen the declarations of scripture that without preparation we would wither in the presence of God; that there must be an overshadowing and protective surrounding in order for us to endure his presence or even the presence of angels?[1]

The fire that consumes need be no different in quality or nature from the fire that hallows, purifies, and heals. A little bit of sunshine clears our complexion. More than that can destroy our very faces. And if we are long in the desert without shade we turn into human cinders.

Of others who now dwell in the spirit world, it is said that "their glory could not be endured [by us]."[2] They are "enveloped in flaming fire."[3] Not, as tradition has it, in the fires of hell, but in the everlasting burnings of heaven.

The fulness of the glory of the Father is defined often as this marvelous presence that is overwhelming. "Our God is a consuming fire."[4]

It is also defined in direct analogy to the statement of the Prophet that in chaotic matter, in element, "dwells all the glory."[5]

Radical implications follow: God and man, spirit and matter, eternity and time, spirit and body, heaven and earth are different in degree—not in kind.

---

1. See Abraham Facsimile no. 2 and the fragmental Egyptian Alphabet prepared at Kirtland.
2. *Teachings of the Prophet Joseph Smith,* 325.
3. *Words of Joseph Smith,* 253.
4. Ibid., 371–72.
5. Smith, *History of the Church,* 6:308.

FORGIVENESS THAT TRANSFORMS

One morning we were on the holy mount not far from the environs of Solomon's porch where Jesus "sat down, and taught them" (John 8:2).

We were trying to recount the incident of the woman taken in adultery. After citing the verse ending, "the first stone," I simulated Jesus reaching down and writing in the sand. Perhaps he turned away from the hostile and baiting crowd, I said, to avoid confrontation and to let conscience do its work.

A ninety-year-old woman was with us. She quietly taught us a line we had never noticed: She observed that the record says the crowd dispersed "beginning at the eldest" (John 8:9). "I am grateful," she said, in effect, "that God is 'an old man.'" Meaning that with age and long, long experience come the deepest wisdom and compassion.

The story as it stands puts Jesus's forgiveness of the woman before any signs of her repentance. Is the record incomplete? Or had a measure of contrition and faith already shaken her soul?

No more powerful stimulus for resolute change exists than authentic, absolute, transparent forgiveness. Someone gauges the worst in you and the divine in you. Someone loves you enough to confide, "You can turn around. I will help you."

The Joseph Smith Translation adds a line that is more than a footnote. It is the very essence of the incident: *"And the woman glorified God from that hour and believed on his name"* (JST, John 8:11).

So, in the presence of his forgiveness and beginnings of healing, can we.

FIVE WAYS TO BE FILLED

Men, women, and little ones in the land Bountiful partook of the sacrament and were "filled" (3 Nephi 18:5). There are many ways to be "filled":

- The appetite is met sufficiently. "Enough, thank you. I'm full."
- One is so absorbed in attention that physical hunger becomes subordinate to spiritual hunger.
- One is filled with the Spirit that lifts and gives utterance.

The Nephite multitudes were apparently filled in all three ways. And in another way, too:

- They were *filled with desire* in prayer: "They did not multiply many words, for it was given unto them what they should pray, and they were filled with desire" (3 Nephi 19:24).

In their midst, Jesus himself prayed, "filled with compassion" (3 Nephi 17:6). Some of the words he spoke could not be recorded. Perhaps these were matters which he has portrayed in modern scripture "only to be seen and understood by . . . those who love him, and purify themselves before him" (D&C 76:116).

They had in a measure been purified in his presence. Now he prayed for even greater purification and unity.

They remembered and recorded, "No one can conceive of the joy which *filled* our souls at the time we heard him *pray for us* unto the Father" (3 Nephi 17:17).

They—and we—can be filled in still another way. We are to pray "with all the energy of heart" for a bestowable blessing: to be *filled* with "the pure love of Christ": love from Christ, love for Christ, love with Christ.

> That ye may be *filled* with this love, which he hath bestowed upon all who are true followers of his Son, Jesus Christ; that ye may become the sons of God; that when he shall appear we shall be like him, for we shall see him as he is; that we may have this hope; that we may be purified even as he is pure. Amen. (Moroni 7:48)

PERFECT IN CHRIST

Jesus once spoke of himself as "perfect." Just once. It was after the fulfillment of his mission—after his Atonement, his resurrection and his glorification. Then he spoke these words to the Nephite multitude: "I would that ye should be perfect even as I" (3 Nephi 12:48). But how in this world amidst the down-drag of mortality can we?

One attainment is within the reach of mere mortals, here and now. The assurance comes through Moroni and his final invitation at the end of 531 pages: He says we can be "perfect in Christ" (Moroni 10:32). Not yet perfect in our imitation of his attributes, but "perfect in Christ"—a relationship.

That can be our blessing in the living present.

Amidst our flaws, failures, and even our lapses into sin and sinfulness, this relationship can endure unbroken and unshaken.

It increases when we recognize that he is holding on to us more surely than we, by covenant, are holding on to him. Also that a full measure of his grace quickened our spirits before mortal birth, and the light of Christ still vibrates in our spirits.

The darkness cannot extinguish it. When Jesus says his light "shineth in darkness; and darkness comprehend[eth] it not" (John 1:5), it means, in one strand, "extinguishes it not" (see D&C 10:58; 34:2; 39:2; 45:7; 88:49). A spark always remains. It accompanies the perfecting process. It is the preface as well as the result of becoming holy. Out of the relationship can grow the completion that now eludes us.

Of this level of righteousness, Joseph Smith wrote, "And above all things, clothe yourselves with the bond of charity, . . . which is the bond of perfectness and peace" (D&C 88:125).

The bond of perfectness is Christ's pure love manifest in his Spirit. It is a perfect bond. It is empowering. And it is strengthening.

OUR INWARD PARTS

"I will put my law in their minds and write it in their hearts" (NIV, Jeremiah 31:33). Another translation says, "In their inward parts."

"Inward parts" in Hebrew *(me'ah)* typically means the place of emotions, the center self, figuratively the place of love.

The Psalmist sings, "The spirit of man is the candle of the Lord, searching all the inward parts of the belly" (Proverbs 20:27). A psalm sings of the Lord, who "healeth the broken in heart" (Psalm 147:3). Elsewhere sacrifices are spoken of as a "broken spirit" (Psalm 51:19).

President Lorenzo Snow taught:

> In all our business occupations we must prove ourselves better than any other people, or we forfeit all. We must build ourselves up in the righteousness of heaven, and plant in our hearts the righteousness of God. Said the Lord, through the Prophet Jeremiah, "I will put my law in their inward parts, and write it in their hearts; and will be their God, and they shall be my people." This is what the Lord is endeavoring to do, and this he will accomplish in us if we conform to his will.[1]

President James E. Faust wrote, "Renewing our baptismal covenants as we partake of the sacrament protects us against all manner of evil. If we partake of the sacrament regularly and are faithful to these covenants, the law will be in our inward parts and written in our hearts."[2]

---

1. In *Journal of Discourses,* 18:302.
2. James E. Faust, in *Church News,* April 11, 1998.

RENEWING AND BEING RENEWED

It is a truism among us that we partake of the sacrament, as we also return to the temple, to renew our covenants. That is needful. It is also sometimes daunting. As President David O. McKay said:

> Who can measure the responsibility of such a covenant? How far reaching! How comprehensive! It excludes from man's life, profanity, vulgarity, idleness, enmity, jealousy, drunkenness, dishonesty, hatred, selfishness, and every form of vice.
>
> It obligates one to sobriety, to industry, to kindness, to the performance of every duty in church and state.
>
> He binds himself to respect his fellowmen, to honor the Priesthood, to pay his tithes and offerings and to consecrate his life to the service of humanity.[1]

No wonder we may feel to shrink. A little voice in us says, "I'd better not do that. How can I ever carry it through?"

But this is the nub of our stumbling block: Until we covenant—which is more than a casual and more or less flippant New Year's resolution—he cannot bless us to keep our covenants—any or all.

Without exception, the Lord appends a divine blessing to each covenant we keep. Every covenant guarantees a response from on high. In the Church of Jesus Christ, well-executed duties expand into privileges, and privileges expand into higher duties.

The most inclusive attendant blessing of the sacrament is his Spirit. The gifts and fruits of the Spirit engulf all our deepest needs: insight, flashes of guidance, energy—all the virtues that center in Christ, and through them all the fire that purifies our feelings and our aspirations.

So, yes, we come to renew covenants. But we also come to *be* renewed—renewed with a divine infusion. Then we increase in strength to honor our pledges with him and with each other.

---

1. In *Millennial Star*, 85:778.

HEARTS CHANGED OR REPLACED?

The story is told of a farm family who became so fond of a piglet they tried to make it their pet. Daily they brought it into the house to bathe, perfume, and clothe it, to make it part of the family. But the instant their backs were turned, the piglet found its way back outdoors into the mire. Finally, as a desperate measure, the family had an operation performed on the pig. They replaced its pig heart with a human heart. From that day on the pig remained in the home and had no desire to leave or wallow.

Joseph Smith taught that "the nearer a man approaches perfection the clearer are his views and the greater his enjoyments till he has overcome the evils of this world, and lost every desire for sin."[1]

Ordinarily we are conduct-conscious to the point that if a man does or does not do certain things we call him righteous. But to cease and desist from sin is not as high a level of perfection as to cease and desist from the desire for sin. Whatever we can do within our own powers of self-discipline, and however by our own bootstraps we resolve conflicts of desire within our own souls, the gospel advocates and promises a mighty change of heart—not by surgery, but by the transforming influence of the Holy Ghost.

The Book of Mormon describes people who, though made of the same dust as all of us, reached a point in their sanctification where they could not look upon sin save it were with "the greatest abhorrence" (see Alma 13:12, 27–28). "Behold," says Nephi, "my soul abhors sin" (2 Nephi 9:49).

In a time of medical miracles when it is in fact possible to repair and even replace the heart of man, this story may lose its metaphorical impact. But the doctrine of sanctification is true, that men's hearts—their center selves, all their being—must replace base desires with a character whose whole desire is to do good. Short of that change, our attempts to live in the imitation of Christ fall short.

---

1. *Teachings of the Prophet Joseph Smith*, 51.

OF GENEROSITY

Acceptance of Christ's Atonement should reach to our nerve endings and generate generosity in us.

In Luke 16:9, Jesus says, "Make to yourselves friends of the mammon of unrighteousness; that, when ye fail, they may receive you into everlasting habitations."

The meaning of *mammon* in Greek is wealth and the confidence of wealth. It means, too, that mammon can lead to avarice and a refusal to share.

Jesus warned about trust in riches. And Paul did not say that money is the root of all evil; he said that "the *love* of money is the root of all evil" (1 Timothy 16:10).

Oliver Huntington recalls, "I heard a brother on one occasion, ask Joseph for an explanation of this passage of scripture [Luke 16:9]. His reply was something like this: 'Man in his existence is as a man on a revolving wheel, eternally changing positions, sometimes up and then down, [and] would not remain forever at the top or bottom, and when a man is up and has plenty he should be liberal and charitable, and the man to whom we are liberal and kind in his day of poverty and adversity may be able to take us into "everlasting habitation" when we are down at the bottom of the wheel where he was when we administered to his necessities,' giving the idea to me, that our eternal existence was full of ups and downs."[1]

Another version of Joseph's statement is:

"Every man will fail sometime. Be charitable and liberal with your substance, for it is only a secondary consideration—the use you make of it is the primary consideration. You may do good to someone who is down today and who will rise and be on top of the wheel when you are down, for every man will fail sometime."[2]

---

1. Huntington, Journal, 2: 209.
2. Huntington, "Sayings of Joseph Smith," 366.

NOURISHING BODY AND SPIRIT

On the first occasion where water replaced wine in the sacrament, the Prophet Joseph records, "At half past five, bread and water were distributed liberally among the quorums, and it was truly a refreshing season to spirit and body."[1] He emphasized to *both* spirit and body. The Savior had made clear that "the spirit and the body [combined] are the soul of man" (D&C 88:15).

Hence the encouragement to come, as did the early saints, bathed, clean of clothing, "Sunday best," in the spirit of temple preparation. They had been admonished, "Cleanse your hands and your feet before me" (D&C 88:74), to clear minds of the concerns and clutter of the work week, and to present themselves with open pores, so to speak, thus becoming fit receptacles for the Spirit.

As for the needs of the spirit within each of us, Brigham Young said: "The Lord has planted within us a divinity; and that divine immortal spirit requires to be fed, Will earthly food answer for that purpose? No; it will only keep this body alive as long as the spirit stays with it, which gives us an opportunity of doing good.

"That divinity within us needs food from the fountain from which it emanated. It is not of the earth, earthy, but is from heaven. Principles of eternal life, of god and godliness, will alone feed the immortal capacity of man and give true satisfaction."[2]

Therefore, we are told of times before when the prophets "did watch over their people, and did nourish them with things pertaining to righteousness" (Mosiah 23:18). They fed them the veritable bread and water of life.

---

1. Smith, *History of the Church,* 2:480.
2. In *Journal of Discourses,* 7:138.

WHO CARRIES WHOM?

Of the ancient children of Israel it is said that they did not hold up the ark of the covenant; the ark held *them* up.

It has been said of those who truly keep the Sabbath, the Sabbath keeps them.

Brigham Young taught, "The kingdom of God on earth is a living, moving, effective institution. We do not carry it, but it carries us."[1]

I have stood atop Masada and then descended to the base where an outdoor amphitheater has been built. In recent times it became the venue for a performance of Mahler's Second Symphony, "The Resurrection." The symbolism was not lost on those who entered. Here, trapped by the ruthless Roman conquest, several hundred zealots made the drastic decision to die rather than submit to pitiless rape, torture, exile, or death.

"An utterly empty victory," some would say. But with Messianic overtones the chorus sings at the climax:

> *With wings I have won for myself,*
> *In fervent loving aspiration,*
> *shall I soar*
> *to the light no eye has ever seen*
> *I shall die, that I may live!*
> *Arise, Yea, thou shalt rise again,*
> *my heart in an instant*
> *What thou hast borne*
> *shall bear thee up to God.*

Even when life seems a losing battle on all fronts and in the last extremity, there is still a way up: Christ.

---

1. In *Journal of Discourses,* 11:249.

THE ADVERSARY AND THE
WORTH OF A HUMAN BODY

Once I had the rare privilege of driving with President Gordon B. Hinckley on the east side of the Sea of Galilee. We looked up to the place known as Gadara. The place of a herd of swine. "What does this narrative tell us?" I asked. "Jesus delivers a boy of evil spirits. Then he permits them to take over the bodies of the Gadarene swine. The swine rush down the clifflike mountain and are drowned.[1] What does it all mean?"

He thoughtfully replied, "The worth of a human body."[2]

The President was echoing the Prophet Joseph: "We came to this earth that we might have a body and present it pure before God in the celestial kingdom. The great principle of happiness consists in having a body. The devil has no body, and herein is his punishment. He is pleased when he can obtain the tabernacle of man, and when cast out by the Savior he asked to go into the herd of swine, showing that he would prefer a swine's body to having none."[3]

We have also been taught that the obsession of the adversary and his hosts is to destroy. Even if they can only retard or, as it were, clip our wings, they achieve their end, to make all men miserable like themselves (see 2 Nephi 2:18, 27). The devil and his aides are the saddest sadists in the universe.

Christ demonstrated power to evict or disperse evil spirits. It is just as crucial that he demonstrate power to prevent their taking possession. When we pray faithfully in his name so may we. How? Our sacramental acts are conjoined in scripture with the promise that they provide armor against "the fiery darts of the wicked" (D&C 27:17).

---

1. See Luke 8:26–39.
2. See Matthew 8. The Prophet taught, "They who have tabernacles have power over those who have not." *Teachings of the Prophet Joseph Smith*, 181, 190.
3. *Words of Joseph Smith*, 60.

THE SPIRIT AND THE SENSES

One cannot see without light. And, instinctively, we are afraid of the dark. Anything or anyone could be out there lurking—someone who can see us when we cannot even see ourselves. Thick darkness is always threatening. The light of the Lord, however, is always reassuring.

The Prophet Joseph taught that the Spirit of God—the light and power of God—permeates all of the senses.

Thus Erastus Snow recalls the Prophet saying that "the Holy Ghost or Spirit of the Lord underlies all of the natural senses, viz., seeing, hearing, smelling, tasting, and touching. This Spirit communicates with the spirit of man, and enlivens all the other senses."[1]

So, instead of desensitizing our eyes, ears, noses, and throats, the Spirit of the Lord enhances, intensifies, and increases all of our perceptual awareness. Inwardly and outwardly it expands the range of our perceptions. It is like opening the lens of a camera, or emerging from fog, or regaining feeling in a hand or foot that has gone to sleep.

Thus to pray and to seek for the blessing "that they may always have his Spirit to be with them" (D&C 20:77), and to the degree that it grows brighter within us, we are relieved of a certain blindness, or deafness, or dullness, or numbness.

---

1. Diary of John H. Standifird, L. Tom Perry Special Collections, Brigham Young University.

CAN THE SPIRIT ENTER A STONE?

Heber C. Kimball often recounted his experience in Chatburn, England, where almost the entire community was converted.

As he went door to door saying good-bye, children clustered around him. An overpowering feeling came over him that he was walking on sacred ground. He took off his hat and felt like removing his shoes. Joseph Smith later explained that ancient prophets had prayed over and consecrated that very place and that Elder Kimball had inherited the blessing.

The rest of his life he counseled the saints:

> Then try it, and see if it will not leave a blessing for us to dedicate our lands. If you think that it will not, never bring another bottle of oil and ask us to dedicate and consecrate it for the benefit of the sick.
>
> I know that we can bless the land, and that through our blessing it will be filled with the Spirit and power of God, and that, too, in great profusion, especially if we are filled with that Spirit ourselves.
>
> Some may call me enthusiastic; but I am no more so than the old Prophets were when they had the Spirit of God upon them.
>
> Let us bless the land we cultivate and the fountains of water, and they will be blessed, and then men may drink of those waters, and they will fill them with the Spirit and power of God.
>
> Let us bless and dedicate the fountains of life that are in us, in our wives and children, and in everything else around us. Can the Spirit of God enter a stone, or one of those posts? Yes; and it can fill every pore as well as it can every pore in my body. Can it enter into my pores? Yes, even into my hair; and it can also enter my bones and quicken every limb, joint, and fibre.[1]

---

1. In *Journal of Discourses,* 5:18.

HOW DO WE KNOW THE SPIRIT IS THE SPIRIT?

"They can tell the Spirit of the Lord from all other spirits," said Joseph Smith to Brigham Young. "It will whisper peace and joy to their souls; it will take malice, hatred, strife and all evil from their hearts; and their whole desire will be to do good, bring forth righteousness, and build up the kingdom of God."[1]

Parley P. Pratt adds: "There is in every man a portion of the spirit of truth; a germ of light; a spiritual test or touchstone, which, if strictly observed . . . will leap forward with a warm glow of joy and sympathy to every truthful spirit with which it comes in contact."[2]

Said B. H. Roberts: "As two flames when brought nearly together seem to leap forward to each to meet the other and blend in one blaze, so the spirit that is in man, being native to the truth, and the inspiration from God leap forward to unite and bear witness of that truth."[3]

And Estelle Caldwell witnesses: "It effects a more perfect union of body and spirit that the spirit may more fully express in action its righteousness."[4]

---

1. Manuscript History of Brigham Young, 1846–1847, February 23, 1847; Church History Library.
2. Parley P. Pratt, in Lundwall, *Masterpieces,* 92–93. Compare D&C 88:40.
3. B. H. Roberts, in *Liahona,* vol. 20, no. 23, May 8, 1923.
4. In *Young Woman's Journal,* 27:691.

CAN THE DEAD SEA BE HEALED?

Ezekiel prophesied, and so have modern prophets, that one day the Dead Sea will be fresh water. It is to become lively and life-giving—healed by water that flows from under the temple.

How can it be?

On a topographical map, the Dead Sea looks like a needle-shaped thermometer. At some places it is 1,200 feet deep. In contrast, the flowing freshwater Sea of Galilee is 250 feet at its deepest.

The Dead Sea is huge. And the land that surrounds it is the lowest point on earth. Buried at the very bottom of the Dead Sea, legend says, is the ancient and corrupt city of Sodom, never to revive or recover. What could be more devastating?

Millions of gallons of the sea evaporate daily under the scorching sun. The saline content is at a maximum. It is ten times saltier than the Great Salt Lake.

So here is wastewater in a wasteland—a veritable dumping ground of all that is stale and an off-scouring, a dirty, degenerate sea at the world's lowest point.

Can anything that sooty, smelly, and useless be regenerated into fresh and sparkling and healthy condition?

The obvious answer is "no way."

And anyway, who would take on that project?

He does. He will.

By analogy, he will take on the depths in us that have absorbed the toxicity of mortality and that defy all other attempts at recovery.

He can purge and purify with living water—because he *is* the Living Water.

IS THERE ENOUGH?

Jesus matched many of his "I am"s with "you are"s. He is:

The Word, the messenger of salvation bearing scripture "in [his] own bosom" (D&C 35:20)
We are to be purveyors of his word
A fountain, never without flowing water
Out of the belly of his true disciples "shall flow . . . living water" (John 7:38)
A vine producing much precious fruit
We are to be his fruitful branches
A light that foils all attempts at extinguishing
We are called to be the light of the world
A gate or door, always open and unlocked
We are to lead to the entryway for many who seek his kingdom
The salt that forever keeps its savor
We are the salt that is the savor of life
The shining truth that frees and is increased by the sharing
We are to be glorified in truth and wisdom, a light set on a hill
A shepherd who never will abandon the flock
We are to reach out to the one and the many and feed his sheep

Christ has sometimes been characterized as a changeless essence, an absolute or static being, a never-moved and never-moving Cause.

We know him as *most moved* in all crucial ways. We can trust his trustworthiness. We know him to be responsive to our first approaches and dependable to the last extreme. He can and does respond, rejoice, manifest himself, intervene, and touch—all manifestations of intimacy. He can be "touched" with the feeling of our infirmities.

This is one more way in which his Atonement is infinite. And why there can be no monopoly in the realm of the spirit. Natural expectations are reversed. There is enough and to spare. Of what? Of everything he has to give, which is everything that really matters to us.

As an artist friend of mine has said, "Perfect is good enough."

PAIN VS. MISERY

"The Son of God suffered unto the death, not that men might not suffer, but that their sufferings might be like his."[1]

Paul taught that we are "glorified together" to the degree that our sufferings are like his (Romans 8:17). That is, when we care most for what he cares most for. (How would it be to care deeply about everybody?)

He came to help us prevent and remove needless suffering. And some of our worst problems and hardships arise from un-wisdom and faulty judgment rather than from overt transgression.

None of us get through life without pain. Sometimes those who often seek to deny themselves of all ungodliness and who turn themselves outward to lift others—even while they themselves are hurting—take on subtler and different anxieties.

But as the prophets resolutely show us, no one suffers as much as the persistent transgressor. Even crossing the plains was for many of the trudging companies not only endurable but even joyful. Looking back many said, "I never felt better in my life."

So Elder Marion D. Hanks sums it up: "In this life pain is inevitable. Misery is optional."

President Jedediah M. Grant wrote:

> It has given me much of trouble, and a great amount of perseverance, to be happy under all circumstances. I have learned not to fret myself. It has taken me a great while to arrive at this point. . . . I want the Saints to live in a way that they can feel happy all the time, and then we shall enjoy the Holy Spirit.[2]

We all know that the Spirit brings joy. The revelation is that joy brings the Spirit. When we are focused on Christlike living—even in the midst of our woes and disappointments—the Spirit flows more freely. And that diminishes, even removes, pain.

---

1. George MacDonald, as quoted in Lewis, *Problem of Pain,* 299.

2. In *Journal of Discourses,* 3:11–12.

DEATH AND DEATHS

The death of the body leads to the grave. But Christ is equally concerned to prevent and overcome another kind of death. Pluralized. Deaths *in* the body and *in* our total makeup.

We recognize, and sometimes refuse to recognize, these in ourselves.

By our own dereliction or neglect, we may decline in intelligence and mental powers.

We may lose or harden our natural God-given affections by courting impulses to hostility and estrangement and callousness. We may atrophy in physical strength.

We may become "past feeling" so that the still small voice is too still and too small to get by the crust we build around ourselves (see 1 Nephi 17:45).

We may diminish and even die to our own creative and procreative powers.

All these add up to subtraction. We can reach the point where we are dead "as to things pertaining unto righteousness, being dead unto all good works" (Alma 5:42).

The Atonement and the resurrection of Christ can render null and void not only some but all these processes of decline, disability, and death.

Jacob made the distinction among his brethren. "Yea, today, if ye will hear his voice, harden not your hearts; for why will ye die?" (Jacob 6:6).

MY POWER LIETH BENEATH

"Behold, I am from above, and my power lieth beneath. I am over all, and in all, and through all, and search all things, and the day cometh that all things shall be subject unto me" (D&C 63:59).

"My power lieth beneath"—a strange thing to say from the heights. Isn't he beyond all that is here below? Isn't he transcendent and by now indifferent to our dilemmas? He answers:

He will leave all the comforts of home to answer our cry.

He can come in and through the location of our darkness and despair.

He comes as a physician intent on cure. Complete cure.

He is adept in treatment of all manner of diseases: of mind, of feeling, of the flesh. Even for the man who said, "I was so low I had to look up to see the gutter."

The constant dirge of the devil is, "Too late, you are too far gone. Sunk below any hope. Forget trying." But the Prophet said, "The spirit is never too old to approach God. All are within reach of pardoning mercy."[1]

For Christ will descend (he has been there before) in mud over his boot tops. If that is not enough, up to his waist. And he will probe lower still into realms "frightful, sheer, no-man-fathomed."[2]

He may be the last person you would expect to meet in a pit and find him looking up at you. He is instead the first. Lower than the soles of our feet.

When he can't pull you up beyond your addictions and vainglorying habits, he will push you up. He will pour oil and wine into your wounds.

He can reach you wherever you are with intent you never recognized, with strength you never gauged, with power.

We all know people who tend to "lord it over" others.

He Lords it under.

---

1. *Words of Joseph Smith,* 77.
2. Gerard Manley Hopkins, "No Worst, There Is None."

ON LUMINOSITY

Wilford Woodruff wrote:

Every substance is surrounded with an atmosphere and in some respects shows what is within.

So there is an atmosphere [which] surrounds all persons, which you feel when you meet with them. Some persons' atmosphere you like, others you do not. With some you feel safe, with others you do not.

It is so in meeting with families. Jesus said when you go into a house let your peace dwell upon it but if they do not receive you let your peace return unto you again. This is true doctrine. (Let my atmosphere be good so that the Spirit of God & good men may dwell with me in peace.)

For that person who dwells near the Lord and has an eye single to his glory can tell whether He has the spirit of God or not when He meets with him. Many bodies are opaque & not luminous but when the light of a luminous body strikes them it sets them all in a blaze. So with one who has the Spirit of God: when his spirit rests upon another it overshadows him. It sets him in a blaze and the great light can see the Heart.

We are all, as it were painters, painting our own characters. . . . When we have painted unto the end of our days our character will be presented before God in its true light & we shall see as we are seen & know as we are known.[1]

---

1. *Wilford Woodruff's Journal,* 4:53.

"PEACE, LOVELY CHILD OF HEAVEN"

Written by the Prophet Joseph under the title, "A Friendly Hint to Missouri":

Jesus said, "Blessed are the peace makers, for they shall be called the children of God"—wherefore if the nation, a single state, community, or family ought to be grateful for any thing, it is peace.

Peace, lovely child of heaven; peace, like light from the same great parent, gratifies, animates and happifies the just and the unjust, and is the very essence of happiness below, and bliss above. He that does not strive with all his powers of body and mind: with all his influence at home and abroad, and to cause others to do so too, to seek peace, and maintain it for his own benefit and convenience, and for the honor of his state, nation and country, has no claim on the clemency of man; nor should he be entitled to the friendship of woman or the protection of government.

But the peace maker, O give ear to him! for the words of his mouth, and his doctrine, drop like the rain, and distil as the dew; they are like the gentle mist upon the herbs, and as the moderate shower upon the grass. Animation, virtue, love, contentment, philanthropy, benevolence, compassion, humanity, and friendship, push life into bliss, and men a little below the angels, exercising their powers, privileges and knowledge, according to the order, rules and regulations of revelation, by Jesus Christ dwell together in unity: and the sweet odor that is wafted by the breath of joy and satisfaction from their righteous communion, is like the rich perfume from the consecrated oil that was poured upon the head of Aaron; or like the luscious fragrance that rises from the fields of Arabian spices; yea more, the voice of the peace maker

> *Is like the music of the spheres,*
> *It charms our souls, and calms our fears;*
> *It turns the world to paradise,*
> *And men to pearls of greater price.*[1]

---

1. Smith, *History of the Church*, 6:245.

WHAT OF IRREVERSIBLE MISTAKES?

One Friday night in Jerusalem I walked with a man who had traveled far to see and stand on these sites.

We followed the probable pathway from the Last Supper room down to the valley of Kidron and then up to the traditional locus of the Garden of Gethsemane.

In the darkness, so I could not see his tears, he volunteered:

> I am a pilot. I married and then trained my wife to be a pilot. One day I took off first, made a pilot error, and recovered. She followed me in the same error, crashed, and was killed.
>
> I could never have recovered from that anguish until the night when it was as if I heard the voice of the Redeemer. "I didn't just die for your sins. I died for your dumb mistakes."

How heavy, how helpless, how hopeless the weight of such tragedies. Accidents happen. And wittingly or not, we can compound hurts and make a shambles of other people's lives.

Such damage is permanent. Must it be?

Jesus asks to stand between us and those we have misled or wounded or brought to ruin. "If you will come to me and if they will come to me, I will take the ashes of your mistakes and misdeeds and plant in them the tree of reconciliation. In due time, which may seem a long time, I will see that all these things consummate in reunion and regeneration and work together for good. Lasting, stinging regret will be swallowed up."

This is to say that through Christ, our hopeless losses need not be hopeless nor losses. "All your losses will be made up to you in the resurrection, if you continue faithful. By the vision of the Almighty I have seen it."[1]

All the king's horses and all the king's men will fail. The King of kings will not.

---

1. *Words of Joseph Smith,* 196.

ADAM AND EVE AND THEOSIS

We are taught that by partaking of "things unfit" our first parents passed through the doors of mortality and in a measure lost touch with the divine realm. Can we reverse the process by taking of things fit?

Milton in *Paradise Lost* describes a correlation between Adam's and Eve's sacramental eating in this world and their eventually attaining *theosis,* or deification.

The same theme appears in the early Church fathers. The central idea is theosis, the assimilation of humankind to God. Such progression toward the divine is brought to pass in part through eating—specifically, eating sacramental elements.

One guide to this transformation is clear in Peter's writings. He speaks of the exceedingly great and precious promises of Christ and says that through the ordinances, we are "partakers of the divine nature" (2 Peter 1:4).

By partaking,[1] accompanied by the Spirit of God, we are preparing ourselves to be sufficiently pure to reenter his presence.

Death came to Adam and Eve; by eating, we can reverse the blows of death and attain a higher and higher resurrection. Food is not the enemy; food is not only what we need but what we are ("we are what we eat"). And what the Spirit is making of us.

If our partaking is "not to excess, neither by extortion" (D&C 59:20), and not idly, and if the food is consecrated, the Spirit is invited in and comes to stay.

We are on our way to a higher and blessed state.

---

1. In Greek, "sharer, associate, companion, partner."

CHRIST BECAME DIVINE

A well-meaning biblical authority said to me, "God's incarnation can be explained thus: It is like someone saying 'I love dogs so much that I will, to help them, become a dog.'"

The analogy breaks down. Dogs may share in the image of creaturely life. But humankind are in the image of God himself. That image was implanted in Christ the Firstborn Son, and in us as spirit sons and daughters. And in Adam and Eve before they or anyone else entered this world. Christ, the preeminent Son of God, came not to *initiate* but to *complete* the image in us.

My four-year-old daughter once said, "Every Mr. or Mrs. Nobody is Heavenly Father's friend." Yes. Because every "nobody" is his child. How hard it seems to us to be equally concerned, as he is, about every one. We impose limits on our love. But he hasn't left that option open for himself. "There is a love from God that is peculiar to itself. But it is without prejudice."[1] "All are alike unto God" (2 Nephi 26:33).

Our recognition of Christ's divine nature excels every attempt at creedal language. We have been taught by Christ himself that if we could see him now in his glorified, divinely perfected body, and in the majesty of his glory, we would recognize what he himself said: "He that hath seen me hath seen the Father" (John 14:9).

He is not identical with the Father. He has become his exact similitude by moving "from grace to grace" (D&C 93:13).

So we affirm the logical couplet: If Christ is like God, then God is like Christ.

And if we are not becoming more Christlike, and therefore Godlike, we are not yet his disciples.

He is trying in every way possible to nourish and perpetuate our growth. "You shall receive of his fulness, and be glorified in me as I am in the Father" (D&C 93:20).

All else is commentary.

---

1. *Teachings of the Prophet Joseph Smith*, 147.

Glimpses Beyond

TO BE CAUGHT UP, AND THEN TO
SIT DOWN AT THE GREAT FEAST

Envisioning these last days of tumult and distress, Jesus promised: "And whoso treasureth up my word, shall not be deceived, for the Son of Man shall come, and he shall send his angels before him with the great sound of a trumpet, and they shall gather together the remainder of his elect from the four winds, from one end of heaven to the other" (Joseph Smith—Matthew 1:37). In the mode of patriarchal assurance, this promise is made personal and vivid:

> You will hear the cry of the great Bridegroom;
> You will look up and see a mighty host with him
>   coming with power and great glory.
> You with your family will be caught up to meet
>   them and the saints.
> You will return with them to that great feast;
> You will sit down with them at the table and
>   partake of its rich bounties there in the
>   New Jerusalem.
> You will see the Lamb of God in the power of his glory;
> You will partake in part of his likeness.[1]

So, as President John Taylor wrote of sacramental worship, "We not only commemorate the death and sufferings of our Lord and Savior Jesus Christ, but we also shadow forth the time when He will come again and when we shall meet and eat bread with Him in the Kingdom of God."[2]

The sacrament is a dress rehearsal for that day of destiny. Thus we approach his very likeness. For "intelligence cleaveth unto intelligence; . . . truth embraceth truth" (D&C 88:40).

---

1. Blessing of William G. Perkins on head of Allen J. Stout. In journal of Allen J. Stout, typed copy.
2. *Journal of Discourses,* 14:185.

THE TEMPLE FEAST

In the midst of "laying the foundation" of Zion in the area of the New Jerusalem (D&C 58:7), a revelation was given. It was the first Sabbath after the arrival of the Prophet in Jackson County, Missouri, August 11, 1831. Of the future supper of the Lord it pledged and promised:

> Yea, a supper of the house of the Lord, well prepared, unto which all nations shall be invited.
>
> First, the rich and the learned, the wise and the noble;
>
> And after that cometh the day of my power; then shall the poor, the lame, and the blind, and the deaf, come in unto the marriage of the Lamb, and partake of the supper of the Lord, prepared for the great day to come. (D&C 58:9–11)

All this is to occur at the center of the holy city and temple of God: a "supper of the Lord. . . . And that the testimony might go forth from Zion, yea, from the mouth of the city of the heritage of God" (D&C 58:11, 13).

This projected future feast is in every way a spiritual feast, involving all the dimensions of soulful awareness and rejoicing. It is also a feast that will be relished and enjoyed in the full physical sense—indeed with a sense-spectrum enhanced, not diminished, by resurrection, a concrete, eventful, and event-filled feast.

It is said that a sacred table is made so by the invitation of the poor. Otherwise it is as if we exclude God and the heavenly hosts.

Strangers we may have been, but on that day we will be strangers no more.

OUR BODIES WILL SHINE

Jesus said: "Then shall the righteous shine forth as the sun in the kingdom of their father. Who hath ears to hear let him hear" (Matthew 13:43).

In anticipation of this bright day, the visionary Daniel wrote: "They that be wise [or those who impart wisdom] shall shine as the brightness of the firmament; and they that turn many to righteousness as the stars for ever and ever" (Daniel 12:3).

On Patmos, John described those who overcome through Christ: "And I will give him the morning star. He that hath an ear, let him hear what the Spirit saith unto the churches" (Revelation 2:28–29).

The morning star and the evening star are the same star. Both defy the darkness. Each testifies of daylight as a vivid memory and as a bright alert to its imminent return.

In the comforting revelation called the "Olive Leaf," the saints are promised that "if your eye be single to my glory, your whole bodies shall be filled with light" and that "there shall be no darkness in you" (D&C 88:67). Exactly what John said of Jesus (see 1 John 1:5).

One can ask: Does anything like this happen in our time?

Our archives give uniform testimony. On many sacred occasions men and women have in reality been enveloped in divine light. Attempts to describe them do not speak of a "nimbus" or a circular halo, as in some artistic renderings. But a sheen of light extends from the face and head and body. As one witness wrote of a temple dedication, "All the leaders looked white, some whiter than others."

In this world, as in the next, there are degrees of glory.

A fore-shadowing, or rather, a fore-lightening of the day to come is in the Doctrine and Covenants: "Ye who are [now] quickened by a portion of the celestial glory shall then receive of the same, even a fulness" (D&C 88:29). And "these are they whose bodies are celestial, whose glory is that of the sun, even the glory of God, the highest of all, whose glory the sun of the firmament is written of as being typical" (D&C 76:70).

WHAT CAN THE SPIRIT DO TO US?

Parley P. Pratt of the Twelve, one of the intrepid leaders and writers of the first generation of the Church, gave his life in two ways: in "bearing the burden and heat of the day," and in martyrdom.

He wrote this summation of the long-term influence of the gospel and the Spirit:

> The restoration of these pure laws and practices has commenced to improve or regenerate a race.
>
> A holy and temperate life; pure morals and manners; faith, hope, charity; cheerfulness, gentleness, integrity; intellectual development, pure truth, and knowledge; and above all the operations of the divine Spirit, will produce a race more beautiful in form and features, stronger, and more vigorous in constitution, happier in temperament and disposition, more intellectual, less vicious and better prepared for long life and good days in their mortal sojourn.
>
> Each succeeding generation, governed by the same principles, will still improve, till male and female may live and multiply for a hundred years upon the earth.
>
> And after death in distant spheres
> The union still renew.[1]

---

1. Pratt, *Key to the Science of Theology,* 167–68.

EARTH ROLLED BACK

Many poets view the grand scenes of nature, down to the tiniest details of color, variety, and symmetry, as symbols of the manifested creative love and care of Christ.

To both poet and prophet there is a longing to regain a relationship with the earth in its pristine state, an earth where, as Christ says, "all things bear record of me" (Moses 6:63).

Thus, Wordsworth wrote, "To every natural form, rock, fruit or flower I gave a moral life. I saw them feel, or linked them to some feeling."[1]

The Prophet Joseph taught that the earth is somehow alive and that its stages of existence are typological of man's: It has been formed, beautified, and given a profusion of plant and animal life. It became most beautiful and even glorious when it became inhabited by the children of God.

But like the human family, it has fallen from its original state and position in the cosmos. It has been baptized with water, and will eventually be baptized with purifying fire. It will die, be resurrected, and will return to its renewed and paradisiacal state (see D&C 88:25). It will be rolled back into the presence of God, a celestial orb, a habitation for celestial beings. Indeed, it will become a revelatory instrument like a mirror of a million images (see D&C 130:7).

Instantly and intensely we will feel at home on this earth because we will recognize—re-cognize—that our homesickness is of celestial origin. God our Father and his Son—celestial personages both—will crown it with their presence.

---

1. Lilley, "Wordsworth's Interpretation of Nature," 532.

EMILY PARTRIDGE ON A HEAVENLY EARTH

After pondering the differences between the spirit world and this earth, Emily Partridge wrote in her journal of a family gathering in the home of Brigham Young:

"He spoke of the power that Christ and the Gods had. . . . His countenance was pure and heavenly. . . . He said, in reply to Joseph Young's question 'What do resurrected beings eat?', 'They eat angels' food.'"

With a twinkle she comments, "We were all just as wise then as we were before."

Then she meditates on the splendor of a paradisiacal earth. "Now due to corruption our pleasures are mixed with pain. . . . If we could only realize that this earth with its pleasures, and its beauties and glories were made for man and when it has been made perfect and its inhabitants become pure, who could ask or desire anything more beautiful or comfortable than what our Father has prepared for his children, right here on this earth?

"We will be as capable of enjoying all the earth affords in its purity as we now can enjoy a large juicy peach."

Through our labors here and now we consecrate the earth by our own consecration to Christ. Thus, "a great deal of the earth's curse can be removed."[1]

---

1. Emily Partridge Journal, 16.

ENTERING HIS REST

The Prophet Joseph Smith taught: "God has in reserve a time . . . when He will bring all His subjects, who have obeyed His voice and kept His commandments, into His celestial rest. This rest is of such perfection and glory, that man has need of a preparation before he can, according to the laws of that kingdom, enter it and enjoy its blessings. This being the fact, God has given certain laws to the human family, which, if observed, are sufficient to prepare them to inherit this rest. This, then, we conclude, was the purpose of God in giving His laws to us."[1]

We can in one sense enter his rest now.

We can reach a point in our fidelity and endurance where he gives assurance of more than light at the end of the tunnel. He can prophetically seal us. The testimony of Jesus is first, that he lives, but beyond that is a second testimony that he has made us his. Then the remainder of our life is not as much probation as a completion of mission. The "if" word is removed from "*if* you are faithful."

Ultimately, to enter his rest is to be prepared to endure his presence. Moses "sought diligently to sanctify his people that they might behold the face of God" and enter his rest (D&C 84:23). But they hardened their hearts and lapsed into idolatry.

Instead, when we have given him our hearts, we fulfill the conditions that will enable us to see his face and know that he is (see D&C 93:1).

"His rest" also means the "fulness of his glory" (D&C 84:24). Joseph testifies of the beginning of his great vision of the degrees of glory, "We beheld the glory of the Son, on the right hand of the Father, and received of his fulness" (D&C 76:20).

---

1. *Teachings of the Prophet Joseph Smith*, 54.

ON BEAUTY AND OVERCOMING

During a world tour, President David O. McKay witnessed a spectacular sunset over the placid, reflecting ocean. He watched in awe until it merged into twilight:

> Pondering still upon this beautiful scene, I lay in my berth at ten o'clock that night, and thought to myself: Charming as it is, it doesn't stir my soul with emotion as do the innocent lives of children, and the sublime characters of loved ones and friends. Their beauty, unselfishness, and heroism are after all the most glorious.
>
> I then fell asleep, and beheld in vision something infinitely sublime. In the distance I beheld a beautiful white city. Though far away, yet I seemed to realize that trees with luscious fruit, shrubbery with gorgeously-tinted leaves, and flowers in perfect bloom abounded everywhere. The clear sky above seemed to reflect these beautiful shades of color. I then saw a great concourse of people approaching the city. Each one wore a white flowing robe, and a white headdress. Instantly my attention seemed centered upon their Leader, and though I could see only the profile of his features and his body, I recognized him at once as my Savior! The tint and radiance of his countenance were glorious to behold! There was a peace about him which seemed sublime—it was divine!
>
> The city, I understood, was his. It was the City Eternal; and the people following him were to abide there in peace and eternal happiness.
>
> But who were they?
>
> As if the Savior read my thoughts, he answered by pointing to a semicircle that then appeared above them, and on which were written in gold the words:
>
> "These Are They Who Have Overcome The World—Who Have Truly Been Born Again!"
>
> When I awoke, it was breaking day over Apia harbor.[1]

---

1. McKay, *Cherished Experiences,* 109.

HOW CLOSE ARE ANGELS?

President Heber C. Kimball taught:

> He [God] is near by, His angels are our associates, they are with us and round about us, and watch over us, and take care of us, and lead us, and guide us, and administer to our wants in their ministry and in their holy calling unto which they are appointed. We are told in the Bible that angels are ministering spirits to minister to those who shall become heirs of salvation.[1]

Parley P. Pratt writes that for the righteous, attunement is often increased at nighttime when the outer self, the body, rests from exertion, and the quiet enables us to hear and feel subtler messages around us.[2] Elder John A. Widtsoe associates spirit world closeness in the heightened proximities of the temple.[3]

Joseph Smith speaks of communion "with the general assembly and church of the Firstborn" (D&C 107:19). He elsewhere explains, with Paul, that these are the worthies who have gone before, and some even yet to come. They are bound to us by the ties and covenants of premortal agreement and preparation. They are permitted to monitor our needs—keenly aware, carefully aware, and lovingly aware.

---

1. In *Journal of Discourses,* 2:222.
2. Pratt, *Key to the Science of Theology,* 119.
3. In *Utah Genealogical and Historical Magazine,* 2: 97.

SOURCES CITED

Ballard, Melvin J. *Sermons and Missionary Services of Melvin Joseph Ballard.* Edited by Bryant S. Hinckley. Salt Lake City: Deseret Book, 1949.

———. "The M. I. A. Slogan." Edited by General Board of the Young Ladies' Mutual Improvement Associations. *Young Woman's Journal* (Young Ladies' Mutual Improvement Associations of Zion) 30, no. 9 (September 1919): 468–73.

Brown, Hugh B. *Eternal Quest.* Salt Lake City: Bookcraft, 1956.

Buber, Martin. *Tales of the Hasidim: The Early Masters.* New York: Schocken Books, 1975.

Caldwell, Estelle. "Latter-day Saint Teachings: Lesson V: The Gift of the Holy Ghost." Edited by General Board of the Young Ladies' Mutual Improvement Associations. *The Young Woman's Journal* (Young Ladies' Mutual Improvement Associations of Zion) 27, no. 11 (November 1916): 690–693.

Cannon, A. H. Journal, April 10, 1893. Church History Library.

Cannon, George Q. *Gospel Truth: Discourses and Writings of President George Q. Cannon.* Edited by Jerreld L. Newquist. 2 vols. Salt Lake City: Deseret Book, 1974.

Clayton, William. Discourse, Nauvoo, Illinois, William Clayton's Private Book, January 5, 1841, 275. Church History Library.

———. *William Clayton's Journal: A Daily Record of the Journey of the Original Company of "Mormon" Pioneers from Nauvoo, Illinois, to the Valley of the Great Salt Lake.* New York: Arno Press, 1973.

Dibble, Philo. Diary. Church History Library.

Faust, James E. "Blessings Flow as Sacred Covenants Are Honored." *Church News*, April 11, 1998.

Freedman, David Noel, ed. *The Anchor Bible Dictionary*. 6 vols. New York: Doubleday, 1992.

Gates, Susa Young. "Editor's Department: Not My Will." Edited by General Board of the Young Ladies' Mutual Improvement Associations. *The Young Woman's Journal* (Young Ladies' Mutual Improvement Associations of Zion) 4, no. 12 (September 1893): 569–72.

Glatzer, Nahum N., and Jacob Sloan. *Hammer on the Rock: A Short Midrash Reader*. New York: Schocken Books, 1971.

Grant, Carter Eldredge. *The Kingdom of God Restored*. Salt Lake City: Deseret Book, 1955.

Haight, David B. "The Sacrament—and the Sacrifice." *Ensign*, November 1989: 59–61.

Huntington, Oliver B. Diary and Reminiscences, 1843–1900. Church History Library.

———. Journal, vol. 2, n.d. Church History Library.

———. "Sayings of Joseph Smith." Edited by General Board of the Young Ladies' Mutual Improvement Associations. *The Young Woman's Journal* (Young Ladies' Mutual Improvement Associations of Zion) 2, no. 8 (May 1891): 366.

Hymns of The Church of Jesus Christ of Latter-day Saints. Salt Lake City: The Church of Jesus Christ of Latter-day Saints, 1985.

Josephus, Flavius. *The Complete Works of Josephus*. Translated by William Whiston. Grand Rapids, Michigan: Kregel Publications, 1960.

Journal of Discourses. 26 vols. Liverpool: Latter-day Saints Book Depot, 1854–86.

Kimball, Heber C. Discourse. Salt Lake City, April 6, 1857. Church History Library.

Lewis, C. S. *The Problem of Pain*. New York: HarperOne, 2001.

Lilley, J. P. "Wordsworth's Interpretation of Nature." *Hibbert Journal: A Quarterly Review of Religion, Theology, and Philosophy* 19 (April 1921): 532–50.

Lind, Don. "The Heavens Declare the Glory of God." *Ensign*, November 1985, 39.

Lundwall, N. B., editor. *Masterpieces of Latter-day Saint Leaders: A Compilation of Discourses and Writings of Prominent Leaders of the Church of Jesus Christ of Latter-day Saints*. Salt Lake City: Deseret Book, 1954.

Madsen, Truman. *Eternal Man*. Salt Lake City: Deseret Book, 1966.

———. "The Savior, the Sacrament, and Self-Worth." Talk delivered at the 1999 BYU Women's Conference. Available at http://ce.byu.edu/cw/womens conference/archive/1999/madsen_truman.pdf.

McConkie, Oscar Walter. *Angels*. Salt Lake City: Deseret Book, 1975.

McKay, David O. *Cherished Experiences from the Writings of President David O. McKay*. Edited by Clare Middlemiss. Salt Lake City: Deseret Book, 1976.

———. In Conference Report. Salt Lake City: The Church of Jesus Christ of Latter-day Saints, April 1946.

———. In *The Latter-day Saints' Millennial Star*, 85 (1923): 778.

Minutes, Salt Lake City School of the Prophets, October 3, 1883, 56. Church History Library.

Moore, Heather B. *Desert Saints Magazine*, June 1, 2007.

New American Standard Bible. Anaheim, CA: Foundation Publications, 1995.

Partridge, Emily. Journal, n.d. Church History Library.

Pratt, Parley P. *Key to the Science of Theology*. Salt Lake City: Deseret Book, 1973.

Quinn, Michael D. "Latter-day Saint Prayer Circles." *Brigham Young University Studies*, 1978, 79–105.

Roberts, B. H. *Liahona: The Elders' Journal* 20, no. 23 (May 1923).

———. Personal Journal. Church History Library.

———. Scrapbook of Georgia Mowry, Ogden, UT, November 21. Church History Library.

Smith, Hyrum. In *Times and Seasons* 5, no. 14 (August 1844).

Smith, Joseph. *History of The Church of Jesus Christ of Latter-day Saints*. Edited by B. H. Roberts. 7 vols. Salt Lake City: Deseret Book, 1932–51.

———. *Joseph Smith's New Translation of the Bible*. Independence, MO: Herald Publishing House, 1970.

———. Minute Book for 1839, L. Tom Perry Special Collections, Brigham Young University.

———. *The Personal Writings of Joseph Smith*. Edited by Dean C. Jessee. Salt Lake City: Deseret Book, 1984.

———. *Teachings of the Prophet Joseph Smith*. Edited by Joseph Fielding Smith. Salt Lake City: Deseret Book, 1976.

———. *Times and Seasons* 3, no. 10 (March 1842).

————. *The Words of Joseph Smith: The Contemporary Accounts of the Nauvoo Discourses of the Prophet Joseph.* Edited by Andrew F. Ehat and Lyndon W. Cook. Vol. 6 of Religious Studies Monograph Series. Provo, Utah: Religious Studies Center, Brigham Young University, 1980.

Smith, Joseph Fielding. In Conference Report, Salt Lake City: The Church of Jesus Christ of Latter-day Saints, October 1929, 63.

Snow, Eliza R. Journal. Church History Library.

————. *Biography and Family Record of Lorenzo Snow, One of the Twelve Apostles of the Church of Jesus Christ of Latter-day Saints.* Salt Lake City: Deseret News, 1884.

Snow, Erastus. Diary. Church History Library.

————. Sketchbook. L. Tom Perry Special Collections, Brigham Young University, Provo, Utah.

Snow, Lorenzo. Office Journal, 1900. Church History Library.

Standifird, John H. Diary. L. Tom Perry Special Collections, Brigham Young University.

Stout, Allen J. "Blessing of William G. Perkins on head of Allen J. Stout." Journal. Church History Library.

Stuy, Brian, ed. *Collected Discourses Delivered by Wilford Woodruff, His Two Counselors, the Twelve Apostles, and Others.* 5 vols. 1987.

The Utah Genealogical and Historical Magazine, 2 (1910): 97.

Whitney, Orson F. *The Strength of the "Mormon" Position.* Independence, MO: Zion's Printing & Publishing, 1917.

Woodruff, Wilford. Journal. Church History Library.

————. *Wilford Woodruff: History of His Life and Labors as Recorded in His Daily Journals.* Edited by Matthias F. Cowley. Salt Lake City: Bookcraft, 1964.

————. *Wilford Woodruff's Journal: 1833–1898 Typescript.* Edited by Scott G. Kenney. 9 vols. Midvale, UT: Signature Books, 1983.

Young, Brigham. *Manuscript History of Brigham Young, 1846–1847.* Edited by Elden Jay Watson. Salt Lake City: J. Watson, 1971.

INDEX

Food, of resurrected beings, 143. *See also* Fasting; Feast

Forehead, name of God and Jesus Christ inscribed on, 31

Forgetting, 58

Forgiveness: for others, 37; obtaining, 46; of children, 51; and forgetting, 58; transformation through, 113; possibility of, 130; for irreversible mistakes, 133. *See also* Repentance

Fruitfulness, 92

Garden of Gethsemane, 7, 10

Garden Tomb, 74

Gates, Susa Young, 78

Generosity, 119

Gethsemane, 7, 10

Gifts, 24

Glory, degrees of, 140

God: accepting inscription of name of, 31; love of, 35, 135; timing of, 48; creation and, 68; presence of, 112, 134; becoming like, 134; children of, 135; entering rest of, 144. *See also* Will of God

Godliness, 76

Gospel, long-term influence of, 141

Grace, 11

Grant, Jedediah M., 128

Gratitude, 53–54, 78

Grief, diminished through Jesus Christ, 16

Haight, David B., 2, 109

Haight, Ruby, 2

Hanks, Marion D., 128

Happiness: of Jesus Christ, 16; of children, 51; on Sabbath, 65; and worth of body, 122; through trials, 128. *See also* Joy

Ha Shem, 26, 27

Healing: of sick, 102; of Dead Sea, 126; through Jesus Christ, 130

Heart: name of God and Jesus Christ inscribed in, 31; potential softening of, 36; offerings from heart of, 40; honest, 42; broken, and contrite spirit, 45; change of, 118. *See also* "Inward parts"

Hinckley, Gordon B., 122

His Righteous Kingdom, 25

Holy Ghost: hearing voice of, 3; song and, 71; enters us during sacrament, 83; as guide, 96; as blessing of sacrament, 117; change through, 118; senses and, 123; identification of, 125; brings joy, 128; presence of, 131; long-term influence of, 141

Hopis, 80

Hour, 4

Huntington, Oliver, 101, 119

Imagination, 39

Ingratitude, 53

Introspection, 47

"Inward parts," 116

Israelites: deliverance of, 5; and Sabbath as banquet, 67; manna given to, 83; and ark of the covenant, 121

Jackson County, Missouri, 43

Jaredites, 73

Jerusalem, 36, 87

Jesus Christ: sacrament as our access to, 2; Simeon holds infant, 3; hour of, 4; as deliverer, 5; gives warnings and reassurances, 6; strength through, 7; as suffering servant, 8; anointing of, 10, 93; fulfilled but did not replace law, 11; joyful nature of, 16;

postpones judgment, 17; represented in sacrament, 22; body of, 23; taking upon name of, 25–26; praying in name of, 28; accepting inscription of name of, 31; always remembering, 32; need for, as mentor and exemplar, 34; self-knowledge and knowledge of, 35; seeking, 40, 48; being shaped by, 45; communion with, 47; teachings of, on children, 50–51; receiving, 53; recognizing, 57; on fasting, 76; birth of, 82; presence of, 85; as anointed and anointing one, 86; as living water, 87; "Lamb" as title of, 91; staying connected to, 92; drinks bitter cup, 95; being filled with pure love of, 114; as filled with compassion, 114; perfection through, 115; infinite nature of, 127; comfort and healing through, 130; divine nature of, 135; David O. McKay's dream of, 145. *See also* Atonement; Second Coming

Jews, and Sabbath as banquet, 67
John the Baptist, 76
John the beloved, 5
Joy: of Jesus Christ, 16; possibility of, 36; on Sabbath, 65. *See also* Happiness
Judgment, 17, 34, 58
Justice, 11

Kimball, Heber C., 45, 104, 124, 146
Kingdom of God, 15, 29, 121
King of Righteousness, 25
Kippur, 12
Kirtland, Ohio, feast for poor in, 100
Kirtland Temple: dedicatory prayer of, 17; instructions on design of, 40; divine manifestations at, 99
Kneeling, 21
Knowledge, promise of future, 71

Kohen Gadol, 25
Kuppuru, 12

Labor, and emblems of sacrament, 88
Lamb, 91
Lands, dedicating, 124
Last Supper: warnings and reassurances given at, 6; prayers given at, 20
Laws, 11
Leavened bread, 84
Lees, 95
Light, emanating from body, 140
Lind, Don, 108
Living water, 87
Lord's Prayer, 15
Love of Christ, being filled with, 114
Love of God, 35, 135
"Love So Amazing," 74
Lower court, 40
Luminosity, 131
Luria, 63

Mahler, Gustav, 121
Malaria, 102
Mammon, 119
Manna, 67, 83
Mary, mother of Jesus Christ, 3
Mary of Bethany, 93
Masada, 121
Matza, 84
Maxwell, Neal A., 109
McKay, David O.: on sacredness of sacrament, 47; on reverence for sacrament, 55; on covenants, 117; dream-vision of, 145
Meeting together, 60
Memory, 58
Mentor, need for, 34
Menuhah, 68
Mercy, 11, 34, 130

154

Sabbath: being at best on, 61; as paradisiacal glory, 62; as bride, 63; observed by pioneers, 64, 104, 105; gladness on, 65; purpose of, 66; as banquet, 67; and finishing work, 68; fasting and, 76; in Far West, Missouri, 101; blessings of, 121

Sacrament prayers: revelation regarding, 20–21; kneeling during, 21; sacredness of, 22; and remembrance of body of Jesus Christ, 23; and unlimited gifts of Jesus Christ, 24; and taking upon name of Jesus Christ, 25–26; and meanings of Hebrew names and titles, 27; and calling on Jesus Christ, 28; blood and, 29–30; and always remembering Jesus Christ, 32

Sacrament table, as altar, 37

Safed, 63

St. Anne's, 70

Salt, 94

Salt Lake Temple, sacrament meetings held in, 106–7, 109

Sanctification: through blood, 30; and change of heart, 118

Satan, 122

School of the Prophets, 99

Second Coming, 96, 138

Security, 13

Seder, 5

Self-discernment, 47

Self-knowledge, 35

Senses, Holy Ghost and, 123

Sepphoris, crucifixion in, 4

Shem, 27

Sick, healing of, 102

Silence, 49

Simeon, 3

Sin: remission of, through shedding of blood, 29; forgetting, 58; desire for, 118; as cause of pain, 128. *See also* Forgiveness; Repentance

Smith, Hyrum, 83, 107

Smith, John, 103

Smith, Joseph: on charity, 12; on knowing people through their face, 17; on kingdom of God, 29; on motive and knowing ourselves, 35; on Jackson County, Missouri, 43; on keeping commandments, 45; on repentance and past sin, 58; on earth in glorified state, 62; on joy in gospel, 65; on caring for poor, 79; on first sacrament of latter days, 98; organizes feast for poor, 100; gives pattern for sacrament, 101; and healing of sick, 102; on approaching perfection, 118; on generosity and ups and downs of life, 119; on worth of body, 122; on Holy Ghost and senses, 123; on identification of Holy Ghost, 125; on mercy, 130; on peacemakers, 132; on celestial rest, 144; on proximity of angels, 146

Smith, Joseph Fielding, 39

Snow, Eliza R., 76, 104

Snow, Erastus, 99, 106, 123

Snow, in Jerusalem, 36

Snow, Lorenzo, 107, 116

Song: as prayer, 70, 73; given in D&C 84, 71, 74; new, of Psalm 98, 72

Sorrow, diminished through Jesus Christ, 16

Space, sacrament in, 108

Spirit: contrite, 43, 45; nourishing, 120

Spiritual death, 129

Spiritual needs, 120

Spiritual orientation, 108

Spirit world, 112, 146

PERSONAL REFLECTIONS

PERSONAL REFLECTIONS

PERSONAL REFLECTIONS

PERSONAL REFLECTIONS

PERSONAL REFLECTIONS

PERSONAL REFLECTIONS